PROPHETIC WORDS FROM THE HEART OF THE FATHER FOR A NATION & A PEOPLE:

IN GOD WE TRUST

2007 - 2011 PROPHETIC WORDS FROM THE HEART OF THE FATHER: FOR A NATION & A PEOPLE: IN GOD WE TRUST - 2007-2011

Cover Art: Richard Croft - w3designteam.com
Editor: Christie Roe-Pride
Cover Photo: Shuttershock

ISBN 10: 0615809251
ISBN 13: 9780615809250

ACKNOWLEDGEMENT

To Ruach HaKodesh (Holy Spirit):

For His faithfulness to teach me to hear His voice
and the heart of the Father

TABLE OF CONTENTS

FOREWORD

This book will go forth for My glory in the land; a voice speaking to My people, a voice in the dark night to wake up those who are Mine. A witness to believers and unbelievers alike, the day of salvation is now. You are not guaranteed a tomorrow, why tempt the Lord your God? Fall at my feet, surrender all; every plan, every purpose, every dream, your will and desires, and watch Me transform your life. Many are in danger. That danger is growing greater every day. Today is the day of salvation. Do not tempt the Lord your God, for no one knows the day nor the hour of redemption or condemnation, for I come as a thief in the night to gather the elect from the four corners. They will worship Me as one voice, in Spirit and in truth. What a glorious day that will be when you see Me face to face. I AM speaking to a people and a nation. Are you listening?

Ezekiel 33:1-9 *Again the word of the LORD came to me, saying,* *[2] "Son of man, speak to the children of your people, and say to them: 'When I bring the sword upon a land, and the people of the land take a man from their territory and make him their watchman, [3] when he sees the sword coming upon the land, if he blows the trumpet and warns the people, [4] then whoever hears the sound of the trumpet and does not take warning, if the sword comes and takes him away, his blood shall be on his own head. [5] He heard the sound of the trumpet, but did not take warning; his blood shall be upon himself. But he who takes warning will save his life. [6] But if the watchman sees the sword coming and does not blow the trumpet, and the people are not warned, and the sword comes and takes any person from among them, he is taken away in his iniquity; but his blood I will require at the watchman's hand.'*

[7] "So you, son of man: I have made you a watchman for the house of Israel; therefore you shall hear a word from My mouth and warn them for Me. [8] When I say to the wicked, 'O wicked man, you shall surely die!' and you do not speak to warn the wicked from his way, that wicked man shall die in his iniquity; but his blood I will require

at your hand. ⁹ Nevertheless if you warn the wicked to turn from his way, and he does not turn from his way, he shall die in his iniquity; but you have delivered your soul.

INTRODUCTION

We attended a church picnic and baptism in 2004. On that day, I had no intentions of being baptized again, but the Lord had other ideas. I did not have it all together when I was baptized the first time, so this was an opportunity to do it right. Almost as soon as I came up out of the water, I was short of breath. By the next morning, I was struggling to breathe and the doctors did not know what was going on. I was on antibiotics and breathing treatments. I could not sleep except for "cat naps," as I was choking on my own saliva. I could speak barely above a whisper; only a word or two before losing breath. Swallowing occurred only in tiny sips, one at a time. This continued for ten months!

Exactly, 21 days into this illness, at 3 am I was downstairs on my knees praying. Listening to worship music I was crying out in my thoughts to the Lord, asking Him to heal me. Without warning, the face of a demon manifested itself in front of me and began to laugh. I can still hear its laugh. People ask me what it looked like. It was bluish in color, with long black curly hair parted in the middle and a mouth that looked like "Joker" from Batman. I whispered, "Jesus help me," and it dematerialized. Shaking and terrified I went upstairs and got into bed. I thought "God, could you not let me see an angel? It had to be a demon? What was that about?" I was afraid to tell anyone at first. I thought that perhaps I was suffering from a lack of oxygen, or maybe I truly was crazy for my sold-out faith as people were saying...Later that morning, I asked, "Lord, you are trying to tell me something, what is it?" I went to pick my bible up from the table and it fell open to the 10th chapter of **Daniel**:

> *Do not be afraid, Daniel. Since the first day that you set your mind to gain understanding and to humble yourself before your God, your words were heard, and I have come in response to them.* 13 *But the prince of the Persian kingdom*

resisted me twenty-one days. Then Michael, one of the chief princes, came to help me, because I was detained there with the king of Persia. ^{14} Now I have come to explain to you what will happen to your people in the future, for the vision concerns a time yet to come."

^{15} While he was saying this to me, I bowed with my face toward the ground and was speechless. ^{16} Then one who looked like a man touched my lips, and I opened my mouth and began to speak. I said to the one standing before me, "I am overcome with anguish because of the vision, my lord, and I am helpless. ^{17} How can I, your servant, talk with you, my lord? My strength is gone and I can hardly breathe." ^{18} Again the one who looked like a man touched me and gave me strength. ^{19} "Do not be afraid, O man highly esteemed," he said. "Peace! Be strong now; be strong."

I picked up the phone and called the office of the church where we were attending. The worship pastor answered. I explained what happened earlier that morning; the demon, the scripture reference, the fact I was ill for 21 days and the scripture reference had mentioned 21 days. He responded, "That was a demon, I have seen those laughing faces before at a Mormon funeral. You are under attack." He offered no other information or support, and I had no idea what that really meant. For the next ten months, this "illness" continued.

It was physically the worst time in my life. I had never been ill like that before. Other than "cat napping," I was awake the majority of the days and nights. Holy Spirit was so faithful; He was there to teach me through the night hours, like a private tutor. Since I could not talk, I could not chat on the phone or dictate work. I had to be silent. Every time I tried to pray during these months, either whispering or in my thoughts, the Lord immediately and firmly cut me off, speaking, "Be still and know that I AM God." Prior to this illness, there was not much quiet time. I was juggling a successful medical legal consulting company, along with devoting time to my marriage, attending church, raising kids, their friends, pets, and keeping our home. Now, I was in bed much of the time. My life had gone from 60 mph to zero in no time. As sick as I was, it was the most amazing time with the Lord!

God began to build my faith. He taught me to hear His voice, and He began to show me there is nothing He can't do. He taught me to obey. He spoke to me in dreams and visions. I did not understand why I was so ill, or the reasons, I was going through what I was going through. However, I did understand that this was a very special and intimate time I had the privilege of experiencing. Every day was filled with excitement about what Lord was going to teach me. I thanked Him that I would walk as the apostles walked. I praised Him that living waters would flow through my belly with such force that they would flow on to all those I come in contact with! Repeatedly, just prior to a prophetic word or a word of knowledge, I would see a vision of Jesus with a large flask pouring water on my head. He was filling me daily. What an amazing time in my life! It has never been topped, nor diminished in value.

The respiratory illness continued. I still could not eat solid food, and could only sip liquids; fighting for every sip for fear of choking. One morning after showering, I stared in the mirror, taken aback by my reflection. As a registered nurse, I knew I was dying. I was anemic. I could not sleep. I could not eat. I told the Lord, "If it is my time to go, then so be it, but I feel there is so much more you want me to do." I walked downstairs to the kitchen, bound and determined to get a cup of broth down even if it took me all day. After warming the soup and sitting, I turned on the TV. The 700 Club was on with Pat Robertson praying for healings. I was hoping I would hear my problem mentioned, I was beginning to lose hope that God would heal me, when at the end of his show, Pat turned and spoke to the co-host, then turned back and pointed his finger at the TV, saying, "There is a woman out there, you are being choked, and this has been going on for months. It is demonic. Take your hands off her throat in Jesus name! Now do something you have not been able to do, swallow." I swallowed! God had demonstrated His power in a dramatic way; He showed me beyond any doubt that He really can do anything and that there is no distance in prayer.

By now, prophetic words were flowing much like supernatural dictation. There was this voice talking to me, telling me what to write down or what to say to people. Everyone around *assured* me that I was going crazy. There was much persecution by my brothers and sisters in the Lord and I was hurting, but understood. I certainly did not feel that anything "qualified" me for this amazing gift. God does not see the external, He sees the heart; He chose a foolish thing to confound the seemingly wise. God knew one thing, I would speak what He told me to speak when He told me to speak.

What I have learned over these many years is that dreams, visions, and prophetic words are like onions; there are many layers of revelation and they transcend time. What I mean by this is, there will be an initial superficial interpretation, but in the days, weeks, months or even years ahead, the Lord will give deeper and deeper revelation. An event will occur, and the Lord will immediately show me a dream, vision, or prophetic word and He will say, "This is that." It is amazing how God works. Just as we can read the same section of scripture and get something new each time, so also are the Rhema words of God. The word of God is timeless, and alive.

This collection of the words point to a people, a nation, and a remnant of God. It is a collection to encourage and uplift, yet also considered a Watchman on the wall, to warn of things to come. God never does anything without first telling His people. In spite of the words of warning, God is God. He never changes;

Psalm 91 assures us:

¹ He who dwells in the secret place of the Most High Shall abide under the shadow of the Almighty.

² I will say of the Lord, "He is my refuge and my fortress; My God, in Him I will trust."

If we dwell in the secret place of the Most High, abiding in the shadow of the Almighty, *if* we say to the Lord that He is our refuge and fortress and in Him we will trust, *then He* will do everything He promises to us in the remainder of this Psalm.

³Surely He shall deliver you from the snare of the fowler And from the perilous pestilence.

⁴ He shall cover you with His feathers, And under His wings you shall take refuge; His truth shall be your shield and buckler.

⁵ You shall not be afraid of the terror by night, Nor of the arrow that flies by day,
⁶ Nor of the pestilence that walks in darkness, Nor of the destruction that lay waste at noonday.

⁷ A thousand may fall at your side, And ten thousand at your right hand; But it shall not come near you.

⁸ Only with your eyes shall you look, And see the reward of the wicked.

⁹ Because you have made the Lord, who is my refuge, Even the Most High, your dwelling place,

¹⁰ No evil shall befall you, Nor shall any plague come near your dwelling;

¹¹ For He shall give His angels charge over you, To keep you in all your ways.

12 In their hands they shall bear you up, Lest you dash your foot against a stone.

13 You shall tread upon the lion and the cobra, The young lion and the serpent you shall trample underfoot.

14 "Because he has set his love upon Me, therefore I will deliver him; I will set him on high, because he has known My name.

15 He shall call upon Me, and I will answer him; I will be with him in trouble; I will deliver him and honor him.

16 With long life I will satisfy him, And show him My salvation."

Our God will bring us safely home, Amen?

God has four purposes for this book. The most important is to make sure each reader is firmly standing on God's Rock of Salvation. The Lord Told me fourteen years ago, He called me to "raise the dead in the pews." He has been using me for several years to combat the counterfeit gospel with the truth of HIS word. Many have become entrenched in a counterfeit gospel, serving another Jesus who condones their sins. Too many are deceived by the enemy, thinking this counterfeit grace message so prevalent in the emerging church is truth. The tragedy is many churches are preaching messages of half-truths and perversions of the word of God. They do not even know they are being deceived. They are sincere in their faith, but they are sincerely wrong. Throughout God's word, we are repeatedly warned of false teachers, false prophets, and wolves. With smooth talk and itching ears, people will not tolerate true doctrine. We must compare what we see and hear with the word of God. HIS word is the plumb line to which everything is measured.

The second goal is to sound an alarm, sharing what the Lord has been speaking to me. Given the events we have been witnessing of late, we see the Bible coming to life before our eyes. The Lord has spoken many things. His recurrent theme is there will be much shaking, and many nations in anguish, not knowing the way out. Too many who claim to be His children have been living like the world. God is calling us to repentance and to His uncompromised truth. He is telling us to keep our eyes fixed firmly upon Him, not distracted by the things we are seeing around us, but distracted we are.

Also, we must prepare ourselves for the tribulations, persecutions, and even martyrdom to come. This is critically important as much of the body of Christ has an escapist mentality, believing we will be raptured any moment. We do not spread the gospel, vote, or do much of anything for the Lord. We believe that God will take care of everything. This escapist mentality is NOT of God but a deception of the enemy to thwart the plan of God. The fulfillment of prophesy is moving at an accelerated pace. There will be a time of relative peace, the Word tells us, but the Lord has warned us not to be lulled into a false sense of security.

Finally, we are called to return to the basics ~ not just of truth, but the commission Jesus entrusted us with which has been lost in the modern church and the majority of mainstream denominations. Jesus told us to preach the gospel and to reach nations. Additionally, He charged each of us to heal the sick, raise the dead, cleanse the lepers and cast out demons, stating, "*Freely you have received, freely give*" (**Matthew 10:7**). We are told signs and wonders would follow us, not to chase them. Many of us do not understand our authority in Christ, therefore we do not feel qualified or equipped to do as Jesus instructed, but God always equips who we calls! Not one man or woman of faith felt qualified, as a matter of fact most tried to disqualify themselves. They all had a reason why they were not the one.

We sit waiting, when all the while God is saying "child I am waiting on you to step into who I called you to be, to step into who my word says you are. Where is your faith? Your focus should be on Me and who I say you are." There is NOT one mighty man or woman of faith – not one – who people did not point fingers at and say, or do the same things that have been done to you. They gossiped about Moses, Mary, Joseph and about Job! There is not one mighty man or woman of faith who did not feel alone or scared or wonder why God would want to use them. There was not one, who did not face an enemy, but they did not get stuck there. They did not let those wrong thoughts, what man said or did stop them. They were determined in their heart they would serve the Lord – not man.

We MUST change if we are to meet the challenges to come, and the rise of evil in the world. Confidence to confront and maneuver the powers of darkness will mean the difference between life and death for many.

The Lord has not given us a spirit of fear; but of power, of love, and of a sound mind (**2 Timothy 1:7**). If we are feeling fear, witnessing the events in the world, then it is time to reevaluate our relationship with the Lord, as He assures us that, *He will keep in perfect peace, Whose mind is stayed on Him, Because we trust in Him,* **Isaiah 26:3.**

The Message Satan Does Not Want You to Hear

Preached During Praising in the Park

Summer 2012

For those who prefer to watch a sermon, rather than read, this sermon can be viewed on our You tube channel, Bear Witness Ministries. The video is titled; *"The Revised Message Satan Does Not Want You To Hear."* The exact url is:

**http://www.youtube.com/watch?v=EO82mNxPlpI&list=UUa1Y_
Uw_pXuSF1D--8q-5Xg&index=13**

THE MESSAGE SATAN DOES NOT WANT YOU TO HEAR

According to an ABC poll, 83% of Americans claim to be Christians. If this were true, our world would be a very different place, amen? How can these statistics be true? God wants me to share truth about this. You may have never heard it before, and some may not want to hear. We are going to videotape this word and post it to YouTube, because so many sitting in and out of the church today are blind to their true condition. They are told, and therefore believe, that words can save them. Thousands go forward to repeat a prayer at mass evangelism events or every Sunday in churches across this county. They are lulled into a false sense of security, believing this prayer gives them salvation.

Statistics demonstrate that only a fraction of those who come forward at mass evangelism events and church services, or even those who feel compelled to say the sinner's prayer, go on to become committed Christ followers. The majority put their faith in the prayer, rather than in Jesus Christ; this is why we have such a huge disconnect between true and false salvation.

In the church today, people will tell you that if a prophetic word is not encouraging, it is not of God. God *is* love. However, He is also truth. When He confronts us and gives us a word of correction it is always given in love, but given nonetheless. God loves us and desires no one to be lost. He is ALWAYS about bringing restoration. Amen?

It seems that God keeps pushing me along the narrow road. He gives me a difficult word to release, and then tells me, *"As it was with Jeremiah, so shall it be with you."* I would venture to say that a majority of pastors would not preach this message; it is not popular today to share something that isn't warm and fuzzy. This message does not condone sin, in fact it flies in the face of the view of God many have today. But, it is truth. Prayerfully, each and every one of us will hear this word of the Lord, heed the warning, and examine ourselves in light of scripture. Let's seek the face of God before it's too late.

Father, I thank You for the words You have for us. They speak a hard truth; a truth we may not want to hear, but we need to hear. This truth cuts through the lies that surround us; lies that we hear preached in churches or on television, as well as half-truths we have come to believe which leave us vulnerable to the enemy's deceptions. The old saying "Truth hurts" applies to the words You have for us here. We thank You for preparing our hearts, and minds to receive Your truth. May the blinders be removed; may we, just like Isaiah, get a glimpse of our true condition in the presence of You, Our Holy God.

We ask God, that You would give us the glimpse; that we would see our real condition, our desperate need for You ~ for a Savior. May we know in our heart of hearts our true standing before You. Lord, do not allow our pride to prevent us from total surrender to You, Your ways, and Your Word. May we understand what Your grace and mercy really mean. May we approach You on Your terms, allowing ourselves to be drawn in by Your love. Holy Spirit, minister to us. Prepare our hearts and minds to hear the truth. Help us truly be reconciled to You, our God.

Ezekiel 33:7-8 [7] *"So you, son of man: I have made you a watchman for the house of Israel; therefore you shall hear a word from My mouth and warn them for Me.* [8] *When I say to the wicked, 'O wicked man, you shall surely die!' and you do not speak to warn the wicked from his way, that wicked man shall die in his iniquity; but his blood I will require at your hand.* [9] *Nevertheless if you warn the wicked to turn from his way, and he does not turn from his way, he shall die in his iniquity; but you have delivered your soul.*

As with everything the Lord gives me to preach, this teaching is something that He first used in my life, which I learned and have been called to pass on to others. I do not determine what I will share with you. Without fail, the Lord gives me a message. This word is no exception. God has a serious warning for those of us who claim to be members of the Christ's body. This word may sound harsh to some, but too many people are walking around with a false security that they truly follow Christ, yet they are in deception. First and foremost, I want you to know that I have lived this word.

I was raised Jewish. We went to Temple. My family and most people I knew did not know God. No one dared to speak the name Jesus unless it was used as a cuss word. I always believed in God, and also believed that every word in the Old Testament was true. I prayed every day. In 1979, I was introduced to Jehovah Witnesses. Since I didn't know any better, and there was no one in my life to explain to me that this was a cult, I followed from a distance. I never fit in. Somehow, deep inside, I had understanding that something was not quite right. I did not believe all of their teaching. Actually, most went in one ear and out the other and they were angry at my constant questioning.

When I was 19, I came to believe in Jesus. God led me to a book that was given me by the Jehovah Witnesses. It showed all the Old Testament prophecies pointing to Jesus and where they were fulfilled in the New Testament. God can truly use anything to reach us! At that point, I was convinced Jesus was who He said He was. I never prayed the sinner's prayer. I didn't even know what that was. There was no internet back then, and I did not know anyone who was a true believer. I prayed all the time and read the Bible. I was church hopping, looking for answers, but not finding any.

I was convinced that something was missing from my faith walk; something that I was not seeing in the lives of people who claimed to be Christian, nor was I seeing it in the churches. I lived in a desert for decades. Finally, thirteen years ago, I broke. The so-called Christian walk I had learned was not enough. If God was God, and His Word was true, then I realized that there HAD to be more. I realized I was not seeing the signs, wonders, or miracles about which I had read about in the Bible. I was not feeling God's presence, nor hearing from Him. I believed the Bible when it told me I would hear His voice and experience Him, yet this was not happening in my life, or so I thought. In retrospect, God was right there.

I repented before the Lord for trying to hold back parts of my life and not fully trusting Him. I wanted Him to break out of the box I kept Him in. I was sick and tired of hearing from people who claimed to be Christians about what He would and would not do, or what He could and could not do. They believed spiritual gifts were not for today but I didn't. I wanted to know the *heart* of The Father. I begged Him to take away my head knowledge and give me heart knowledge of Him. I wanted to serve the huge God of the Bible; the one who parted the Red Sea, healed the sick, and raised people from the dead. I desired to serve Him on His terms, not my own. As I cried these things out to Him from the depths of my soul, it was then when I truly became "saved." Three years later, I was baptized by Holy Spirit. I was flooded with revelation and could see more truth than I had ever imagined. I could discern the lies which I had come to believe from teachings I had received. I began to prophesy and speak in tongues. Looking back, I can see that from that point forward, there was a huge price to pay. However, I wouldn't change a thing. When I say this message is personal, it is! I have lived it. Praise the LORD that He is faithful!

Father, I come before you now, in the Name of Jesus...You know everyone listening (reading this book). You brought them to it. You know those who are posers and those who are truly Your children. You know every heart. You know those whose hearts belong to You, and those reading this sermon who are deceived; so sure they are saved, but actually on the road to destruction and damnation. From Your word, we know You alone have the power to save. We also know that You do not desire any of us to perish. I pray that You receive great glory as You produce life from our hearts of stone. I pray that You give each of us, including me, an Isaiah moment, and instill in us the fear of the Lord. May Christ's will become precious and consuming to us. Father, You commissioned this word to be used to resurrect the dead in the pews, through the power of Your Spirit. I pray that Your will be done, in Jesus name, Amen.

Preaching is a dangerous thing. If what I tell you today is not true, I am in big trouble according to Ezekiel 33 However, if what I tell you is true, it is God's truths being spoken through me, and your challenge with it will not be with me, the messenger, it will be between you and God. As this word goes forth, each person must determine for him or herself if what I am telling you is the truth or a lie. I stand in faith, believing that you will know in your hearts that these words are not from me. If you decide these words are truth, then you have a responsibility to receive them and embrace God's word.

One of the biggest dangers on Christian TV, and in many pulpits across the nation these days, is the teaching and preaching of psychobabble, biblical half-truths, and even blatant lies. For those who take what is preached at face value, not investigating the word of God for themselves, a half a truth is a dangerous thing. Half-truths are lies, they always leave us with a blind side that misses the mark. We quote scripture all the time, but often when we do, we take the encouraging half of the verse and ignore the rest, or we just quote the verses that we like.

God IS Love. HOWEVER, He also *hates* sin and wickedness. There are many things we choose to do each day that God hates, yet He still loves us. We are called to renew our minds in His Word so that we will have the mind of Christ. He tells us we are to love the things He loves, and hate the things He hates...but do we? God is love, grace, and mercy. He is also justice and judgment. He tells us repeatedly we are not to be like the world; we are not to be like the majority of those who claim to be Christians. The ways of the world are backward from the ways of God. God does not want us to dress, speak, or behave the way the world says.

God does not want us loving sin, wickedness and rebellion; He desires us totally surrendered to Him. He does not want us to pick and choose what parts of His Word we will believe or which parts of our lives we will allow Him to access, yet this is what we do. We think certain passages of scripture do not really apply to us, or we point toward those around us who are walking in ways that are out of agreement with Truth in order to justify our own behavior. When we compare our lives with the lives of others who claim to be Christians, we think we are okay in God's eyes *because we are not as bad as they are.* But, our standard is not how we compare to others. The Bible tells us to examine ourselves in the light of scripture. In **2 Corinthians 13:5**, Paul exhorts us, *"Examine yourselves, whether you are in the faith; prove yourselves,"* yet we rarely compare our lives with the Word of God because it is often convicting. We feel so much better about our choices when we compare ourselves to others. We think to ourselves, "I may be sinning, but at least I am not sinning the way so and so is,"...or, "I may not be doing what I am supposed to be doing" and we point our fingers and say; "but *at least I am not as bad as they are.*" We get a false sense of security in this. Our standard needs to be God's Word, *not* comparison with the world.

While I was in college, some of the professors graded on a bell curve. There were two of us who made others mad after every test because our results threw off the curve. We achieved A's, which meant the vast majority pulled off C's or lower. God does not work this same way; His standard is holiness. He does not "grade" on a bell curve. We do not fully understand holiness, and we have no idea what it means when God is pronounced a *Holy* God. We try to make ourselves feel better by thinking God's grace covers our willful sin; that He grades on a bell, rather than an individual basis.

We may rationalize that we are safe because we said the sinner's prayer, but often we choose to continue our journey on the broad way that leads to destruction, never making a transition to the narrow road. Poll after poll finds little difference between the viewpoints and behaviors of those who claim to be Christians and those who do not. Abortion and divorce statistics, for instance, are the same both inside and out of the church. Statistics tell us up to 92% of people in this nation claim to believe in God, and 83% claim to be Christians, yet only 5% subscribe to a biblical world view.

Why is there disconnect? Let me ask you, how do you know you are really saved? Is it because someone told you that you were, or do you feel confident because you said a prayer? Maybe you believe you are saved because you were baptized as an infant. The modern American church has reduced salvation to a magic formula; just answer yes to a series of questions, recite a simple prayer, and be "saved." People clap and churches brag about how many came to salvation...but it's often nothing more than a than a lie which promotes a false sense of security.

What we do not understand is that we truly have to repent meaningfully; we must have a heart change, be "born again," evidenced by a change in lifestyle that displays fruit of the Spirit. We can deny the Holy Spirit as an inconvenient God. We can deny His gifts and His role in our Christian walk. We can choose to just say a prayer, believing this means we have been born again, but this is deception.

I watched a video of Pastor Paul Washer, who stated that faith, for many, is nothing more than a creed. A creed is defined in the online dictionary (*Dictionary.com*) as 1. any system, doctrine, or formula of religious belief, as of a denomination. 2. any system or codification of belief or opinion. People who have put faith in a doctrine, denomination, opinion, formula of religious beliefs, or recitation of prayer, are going to hell every day. Churches want to be "seeker friendly," and the emergent church is presenting a diluted gospel. Occult and New Age have invaded the churches, which are afraid to offend the populace. Churches today desire to keep us engaged and entertained rather than focused on deepening our walk with the Lord. Their plan is to tolerate everything by slapping the Name of Jesus on it. However, that is not loving. In an effort to keep it simple, encouraging, and entertaining, churches have perverted grace. They have removed the true power of God's transforming fire, all in the name of love. Tolerance is not love. Jesus never tolerated sin. He urges us to go freely, but *sin no more,* once we have encountered Him.

We promote clichés, half-truths, and even blatant lies, rather than telling the whole truth. Pastors are communicating to people that they are saved just by reciting a prayer. We should fear for those who tell people they are saved by saying a prayer...believing there is nothing more to salvation. The Word tells us repentance is required, yet I often hear pastors preach that we do not have to repent. God alone assures people of their salvation. His Spirit will bear witness with our spirit. God is the only One who sees the hearts of men.

Jesus told us in **Matthew 7:13**, *Enter by the narrow gate; for wide is the gate and broad is the way that leads to destruction, and there are many who go in by it.* We hear the first part of the verse quoted all the time; it sounds simple enough. We like this part, even though we really do not understand the full impact of the statement. However, we do not like the last half, so we don't often share that scripture which states, *Because narrow is the gate and difficult is the way which leads to life, and there are few who find it.* We do not want to talk about the inconvenient fact that Jesus said the way is narrow, difficult, and few find it. Those words do not make us feel good; especially if we assume that because we said a prayer of relinquishment, we are automatically translated from the broad to the narrow road without further challenge to our hearts and minds.

The gate, of course, is Jesus. We speak often, both inside and outside the church, about *coming to Jesus*, or *coming to the cross*. We know many do just that. Many come to the gate; they come to Jesus. Most know of Him, claim to serve Him, and claim He is Lord of their lives. However, there is one glaring problem, just responding to Jesus' call does not save us. The rich young ruler came, but he refused to follow. Obviously, there must be more than just coming to Jesus. This choice to respond marks only the beginning of our journey.

We promote clichés, half-truths, and even blatant lies. Jesus taught that after we go through His gate, the *way* is narrow. Way is defined by the Merriam Webster Dictionary as: *a method, plan or means for attaining a goal, a direction or vicinity.* This suggests that we have to do something more than come to the gate and gaze upon the narrow road. I have preached about a vision the Lord gave me of people stuck; fixated on the cross, but never moving beyond it. We must actually move along the narrow way, beyond the cross, to attain the prize in Christ Jesus.

Jesus declared that the way is difficult. The Bible warns us repeatedly that a servant is not greater than his master. When we read of the hardships Jesus endured, and we look at the lives of the Apostles and their persecution, we must expect that our walk will be difficult, too. They were jailed, beaten, and martyred. The disciples who followed Jesus were persecuted and murdered in the coliseum in Rome. Some were dipped alive in candle wax and lit on fire in the gardens of Nero. Back then, it was obvious that the way was difficult; for many around the world, the dangers are real even now. I have a friend, Davide, who lives in Gambisara. They regularly try to kill him for bringing Muslims to Jesus. In this country, we have some stressors, but other than an isolated incident like Columbine High School in Colorado, where kids were killed for their faith, our lives usually are not in danger...at least not yet. Persecution for faith will be coming to the United States. Knowing what you know about your own faith journey right now, will you be able to stand when persecution assails you?

Jesus said the way is difficult, and because it is difficult he said *few* would find it. If we have been a believer for any length of time, we know that even fewer still are willing to walk that difficult road. Many bail when the going gets tough. **Matthew 13** attests, Then he told them many things in parables, saying: *"A farmer went out to sow his seed. ⁴ As he was scattering the seed, some fell along the path, and the birds came and ate it up. ⁵ Some fell on rocky places, where it did not have much soil. It sprang up quickly, because the soil was shallow. ⁶ But when the sun came up, the plants were scorched, and they withered because they had no root. ⁷ Other seed fell among thorns, which grew up and choked the plants. ⁸ Still other seed fell on good soil, where it produced a crop—a hundred, sixty or thirty times what was sown. ⁹ Whoever has ears, let them hear."*

Few are willing to obey God's voice. They are worried that they will be embarrassed or people will make fun of them. This may happen. Many claim to be Christian, but being a true Christian comes with a cost. Few are willing to pay the price that comes with standing up for God and His word. To take a stand for truth, the price is high. Many have been bullied into silence or political correctness; deceived by the enemy and mistaking tolerance for love. Nearly every kind of sin is tolerated within our churches, in the name of love. We do not want to offend anyone, but apparently we are okay with offending the God we claim to serve. We need to be sure we are clearly demarking between loving the person and hating the sin...not just accepting the sin because the person is struggling and desires to be a Christian.

When we confront sin, we are quickly accused of judging. However, God's love is not about tolerance. Jesus never tolerated sin. He confronted it. He showed mercy for sin, but repeatedly told us to sin no more. The apostles spoke blunt truth; they never tolerated sin in their midst from ones who claimed to be followers of Jesus. All were held to God's standard. How can we forget Annanias and Sapphira, who, in the book of Acts, dropped dead for lying?

Grace was never an excuse or license to live or sin as one pleased. Paul told us in **1 Corinthians 5:12**, *What business is it of mine to judge those outside the church? Are you not to judge those inside? 13 God will judge those outside. "Expel the wicked person from among you."* He said we are not to judge outsiders...those outside the church, the ones we tend to think it is okay to judge. However, the ones we think we should not judge, those who claim to be our brothers and sisters, we are called to judge. The very same chapter in which we are called to "judge not," we learn about the narrow way and hear that we will know those who are truly of God by their fruit.

When we look inside churches today, and at the lifestyle of so many who claim to be followers of Jesus, we see the opposite of what we would expect. Many are on the broad road. Fruit is bruised, moldy, and rotten. People are living like the world; talking and acting like those in the world. They are carnal Christians. Carnal, as it is used by the American church, is a term that promotes an excuse for sin. We hear people state that the person walking in overt sin is a carnal Christian. I am here to tell you there is no such thing as a carnal *Christian*; at least not as it is used today. That is a lie from the enemy. One cannot live in sin, display no evidence of fruit of the Spirit, and be a Christian. In **Romans, Chapter 7**, Paul pronounces that he is carnal, stating *14 For we know that the law is spiritual, but I am carnal, sold under sin. 15 For what I am doing, I do not understand. For what I will to do, that I do not practice; but what I hate, that I do.* **Romans 8:7 follows**, *Because the* **carnal** *mind is enmity against God; for it is not subject to the law of God, nor indeed can it be.*

Carnality is a lie that leads us to believe that we are still on the path to life in Christ. I am not sure who defined the term as it is used today, but I am confident it has become America's churches' way to explain, or make excuse for, the condition of the people in the pews. It has become a way to make sin more palatable and more tolerable in the church. This is a self-defeating lie which avoids the responsibility of confronting sin in our churches. Every so called *carnal Christian* is on the fast track to hell, yet nobody has the nerve, let alone the love of God, to speak truth and rebuke the lies of the enemy, snatching this person up from the fires of hell.

People are saved by believing and trusting in Jesus Christ. Mere words or prayers cannot save us. Nor are we saved because we answered yes to a series of questions at some point in our lives. If we are not walking in Biblical truth and assurance, we are not assured of salvation. Recitation of a sinner's prayer is not found in the history of the church, but it is how we have done evangelism since the 1950's. This is one reason many people believe they are saved, who are not.

The majority, both outside and inside the church, will tell you they have trusted in Jesus. However, when you look at their lives, they have the same desires of the world; there is no evidence of Christ's Spirit working within them, bringing them to conviction and repentance. It is not in their dreams goals, or passion. Nor is it evidenced in their talk, or desires and wants. The only visible difference between these people and the world at large is that they attend church regularly on Sunday. When you ask a person of this caliber about their faith, they will express to you that it is none of your business, or they will demand that you stop judging them. Often they will assert that they prayed the sinner's prayer. When you ask about the confidence of their decision for Christ, it will be seen to be superficial. They are trusting in a rote prayer, not Jesus.

There are others who believe they have been saved, as they attend church and seem to bear fruit for a while...but then step off the path and go back to living like the world. As we witness these behaviors, we ask ourselves what happened? We wonder if they are backsliding or perhaps have lost their salvation. It is more likely that their understanding never went deep enough to penetrate their hearts. Scripture talks about seed that falls on rock, withering away because it lacks moisture after sprouting. It also refers to seed that fell among thorns, and the thorns sprang up and choked out the plant. More than likely, these people were never saved in the first place. They knew of Christ, but they never really *knew* Christ; their faith was imitated from the start, never penetrating.

Some people we see every week live relatively moral lives, remain in church, and have a bit of religion but no passion for God. They are stagnant, never growing in the things of the Lord. There is rarely conviction for their sins and change of direction. They can be religious yet not weep or have remorse for things in their lives that do not line up with God. They feel no need to repent over their sins. People in this position are often more concerned with the man or woman behind the pulpit then the actual Word of God. We hear them sharing, "My pastor says this, my pastor says that," idolizing men and ministries versus God, or focused on looking good and spiritual, but unconcerned for the things of God. They are what God calls *the dead in the pews*, and our churches today are full of them. We cannot rely on saying a sinner's prayer without a true encounter with Jesus which moves our hearts and minds.

Some might say I am judging. Others may feel themselves becoming angry. How do I know these people are not saved, you question? I do not have to prove they are saved or not, because they can do that all by themselves. Although they claim to have walked through the gate onto the narrow road, they are still on the broad way. Their lifestyle never changes, there is no heart change, and there is no renewal in their mind. Fruit of the Spirit is not visible in their lives, and they continue to live as they always have done. It will be their own words and lifestyle choices that will condemn them when they reach judgment day.

How many people tell you they know that they are saved because they believe in Jesus? It is not enough to just believe; the word tells us that even demons believe and tremble. Truth be told, demons are more spiritual then many who claim to be Christians today. Many express belief, but do not tremble at the majesty of God. There is no fear of the Lord; God is not precious to them. They are not able to glimpse, as Isaiah did, their true state of being face-to-face with a Holy God. God becomes their good luck charm or BFF (best friend forever), but He is not *Lord* of their lives. There is no evidence they have passed through the gate and are living in the narrow way. They may be convinced that their recitation of a prayer acknowledging sin has saved them...even to the point they will argue that they are just fine, yet they may be far from justified, sanctified and blood bought.

Matthew's Chapter 7 warns us to beware of false prophets. That applies not just to pastors, teachers and prophets, but also to any one influencing our Christian life. A true friend is one who tells you the truth even at risk of making you angry. I have nothing to gain making you angry. If I were seeking money, fame, crowds and security, I would not speak hard words. I would adjust my sermon to share the parts that would speak to you of everything your heart desires, but I am not a "tickle your ears" preacher. I love souls. I cry out for souls. My heart breaks for the state of our "church" and our nation.

I've come to preach a word from God, as a voice crying in the wilderness; a watchman on the wall. We know from many past words the Lord has been speaking through me and others that judgment is coming to the churches. It is a judgment upon false doctrines, bad fruit, and those who preach half-truths and lies. It stands against those who speak only what people want to hear. We have created a god in our own image; one who tolerates, condones and makes excuses for sin.

Many of you are angry right now. You are thinking I am crazy and overreacting. You are mulling over the scriptural truths of *Judge not lest you be judged.* However, as I stated already, the same chapter that says this also talks about the narrow way to Life in Christ being difficult, and few finding it. This chapter also expresses that we will know who are Christians by their fruit. We will know who is saved *by the way they live,* not by what they say! How can we assert that we know what is in someone's heart? Only God can see the heart, but we do not have to see, we can judge through scripture which reminds us...*out of the abundance of the heart the mouth speaks* (**Luke 6:35, Matthew 12:34**). God's Word also shares that we will be *judged for every empty or careless word* (**Matthew 12:36**) on judgment day.

Some say you can't judge a book by the cover, but Jesus asserted that we could. He explained in **Matthew 7:16-18**, '16 *You will know them by their fruits. Do men gather grapes from thorn bushes or figs from thistles? 17 Even so, every good tree bears good fruit, but a bad tree bears bad fruit. 18 A good tree cannot bear bad fruit, nor can a bad tree bear good fruit.* Our behaviors may not

34

reflect the intentions of our hearts, yet our hearts represent who we are and overflow into how we speak. When Jesus enters our heart, He changes our entire being. When we believe we love Jesus and are surrendered to Him, it only makes sense that His love and power will affect every part of our life. If we are driving a car that gets hit by a truck, there will be evidence of that encounter; how can we have an encounter with a Holy God, the God of the universe, an omnipotent, omniscient, omnipresent God and have no evidence of that encounter? He said we will know believers by their fruits. A true God encounter will produce evidence; there will be fruit of the Spirit, renewing of the mind, true repentance and a transferring from the broad road to the narrow road in life.

Sadly, in many there is never a heart change; there is no renewing of the mind, no true surrender, and no real relationship with God. These people are trusting in false security and are not saved. They have not experienced an encounter with the Holy One. They continue living the broad way, no different from the world, without transformation or power. They talk and act just like the world, except that they are religious and go to church. The Lord showed me that these "believers" are deceived by a lying spirit which has convinced them that their empty religion and ritual has saved them. They believe in performance ~ external appearances and saying the right things. They do not understand the Truth.

Jesus and the apostles were brutal. They were blunt with their words. The Jesus I read in God's Word, was pretty darn bold and people got insulted. Paul, James and Peter were the same; they spoke harshly, saying such things as *brood of vipers, get behind me Satan, Hypocrites!* Jesus even made a whip and used it to drive moneychangers out of the temple. He did not do and say this to the world, He was this way with the church of the day. All who followed Jesus closely spoke the hard truth, with compassion, to everyone they met. That, my friends, is real love!

Real love is not lies, compromise, or distortion of truth in order to keep peace. We do not condone sin, thereby loving people into hell. To the contrary, we speak truth and love people to life. No one accused Jesus, or the apostles, of not being loving. What if they came and said some of those very same things in our churches today as they said in the Word? I am convinced if Jesus or the apostles showed up in our churches today, declaring many of the same things recorded in the bible, they would not be recognized, nor would they be accepted. They would be accused of judging or not walking in love, because the church has a wrong definition of love. Paul said in 1 Corinthians that we are to judge those inside the church, the ones who claim to be members of the body of Christ. However, we judge outsiders and turn a blind eye within the church, making excuses for people's sins. These are the wolves among the sheep, tares among the wheat, and they make the church look bad. Their behavior, when accepted, leads thousands down the broad road that ends in the fires of hell.

Jesus said, *"Why do you call me Lord, and do not do what I say?"* (**Luke 6:46**), We need to be doers of the word and more. Going back to **Matthew, Chapter 7**, it also stated, *Jesus said that many will say in that day "Lord, Lord, have we not prophesied and cast out demons in Your name, and done many wonders in Your name?"* *23 And then I (Jesus) will declare to them, "I never knew you; depart from Me, you who practice lawlessness!"* Many have heard me share these words dozens of times; I have not been able to shake them for past few years. His words of condemnation make me cry. Too many will hear them and be astounded.

These people were sincere in their service to the Lord. They were doing powerful things in His name, but they were sincerely wrong. All of their sincerity will not get them into heaven. Everything they have done in the name of Jesus will do nothing but land them in hell. There is no way to make changes, nor are there restarts at that point in time; it will be too late.

It is true, everyone who believes in Christ is saved by this faith, but how do we know we truly believe unto salvation? We can walk around any park, and even any city, and many of the people will tell us they are saved and going to heaven. Yes, it is true; if we are truly born again, the power that saves us is the power that keeps us, but how do we know we truly have experienced true belief?

The scripture teaches the only way for a man to be saved is to pass through the small gate, which is Jesus. To trust Him in faith, that there is no other means of salvation, no multiple choice, no "all roads lead to God." The evidence that we truly passed through this narrow gate is that we are remaining on the narrow path of life. Our belief in Jesus has tangible evidence in the form of transformed life which is being conformed to the will of God. We are obedient to His word. We are repentant and have experienced a change of heart. We have gotten a glimpse of our need for a Savior, and fallen to our knees in gratitude that He is welcoming us to His Lordship.

Isaiah 6:5 reflects. "*Woe is me, for I am undone! Because I am a man of unclean lips, And I dwell in the midst of a people of unclean lips; For my eyes have seen the King, the Lord of hosts.*"

Isaiah got a glimpse of his true self, in the presence of a Holy God, and he trembled. He broke. The question to me is not whether you know God. The question should be *does God know you*? As we as wind down, I would like us to listen, *really* listen, to the word the Lord dictated to me;

"There are a lot of people going their own way, trying to achieve salvation by the works of their hands. They sit in church, they may even call upon My name, but they know Me not. They may say or do the right things, but I know them not, and the number of people who claim to know Me is staggering compared to the number of people I know. The remnant, the true followers, are but a fraction of the number who claim to be My children. Many are on the road to hell and do not even know it. Lying spirits, pride, and arrogance have blinded them to their true condition. They refuse to surrender, preferring to live like the world with a little bit of Jesus thrown in. This is why My church is impotent. This is why signs and wonders do not follow. This is why they know Me not, and I certainly, in that day, will tell them, *"Depart from Me, I never knew you."* On the slippery slope to hell, they care not, but they will care one day. For many it will be too late; doomed for eternity. My voices are crying out in the wilderness, sharing truth that will set them free, but they are deaf to the call; unable to discern truth from lies, thinking they know best.

You can tell them nothing, and the world spins into the future. Time is short, but you love the world and the things of the world more than you love Me. Pretenses are there. Pharisees act of piety and religion, but I do not look at outward appearances,. I look at the heart. I know each man's heart, and hearts are far from Me. I hold your heart in my hand; I control your next breath. The universe fits in the palm of My hand, yet you fear Me not.

You are not taught about My holiness. There is no fear of the Lord in teachings today. I AM a rabbit's foot to bring you luck; a blessing. You take Me out when it is convenient; you rub my foot and make requests. It is a game called life, and most do not see the gravity of their situation. I AM a holy God. I will not tolerate sin in My presence. In that day, many will cry out *"Lord, Lord did we not do this in your name?"*

I will tell them the truth, *"I never knew you."* Words and actions are cheap; man can be fooled by outward appearances, but I cannot be fooled, and your heart needs more of Me, less of man's wisdom. It needs more of My presence.

Surrender to Me, this day; you know who you are. I AM convicting you right now. Stop the games Stop pretending and surrender to Me. Stop holding back and making areas of your life off limits to Me. Bring down the walls. If you say you can trust Me with your salvation, then why can't you completely surrender to Me? I AM waiting. I desire none to be lost. I AM opening your eyes to expose the false sense of security that has come over the body who claims to be in Christ.

The Bible makes it clear that those who are genuinely saved are righteous and holy. They still sin, but with decreasing frequency. A true believer hates his sin (**Romans 7:15-25**) and repents of it. He hungers and thirsts for what is right, and will please his Lord, for it is his reasonable service. He is obedient to God, yields to the leading of Holy Spirit, hates evil in the world, and loves his brother and sister. How can we be a Christian and continue living the way we did before he knew Christ? Making a decision as a child, or being baptized as an infant; saying the sinner's prayer, walking down an aisle, kneeling at the altar, and reading a tract, are not biblical criterion for salvation. We should be daily dedicating and reaffirming our relationship with the Lord. Repentance is not a one-time thing. It, too, is a continual process. What is our life like right now? If sin characterizes our life, there is a great possibility that we are not a Christian at all.

There must be evidence in our lives that we are on the narrow way. When we ask you about the confidence of your salvation, instead of saying "I prayed a prayer," you should be able to express from the depth of your being, "I am surrendered and trusting Jesus. I can see and feel Him working the changes He has made in my life. I sin less and desire the things of the world less. He replaced my heart of stone with a heart of flesh, tender for the things of Him. His heart beats in my chest and His breath flows through me. I have come face to face with my sin and wept. I see my need for my Savior. He disciplines me as His child. I have struggles, but there is progressive victory over sin. There is evidence of fruit in my life, and I am making progress." If we step off the narrow way, Our loving Father disciplines us and brings us back, **Matthew 7:19** says, *"Every tree that does not bear good fruit will be cut down and put in the fire."*

Yes, God disciplines those He loves. He disciplines His children like every good Father. **Hebrews 12:6** explains, *" For the Lord disciplines those he loves, and he punishes each one he accepts as his child."* This is reiterated in **John 15:2** *"He cuts off every branch of mine that doesn't produce fruit, and he prunes the branches that do bear fruit so they will produce even more."* It is not just the enemy who comes after us to edit the call of God on our life, it is also God who disciplines and prunes us. He puts us on the potter's wheel, then molds and shapes us into the image of Christ. This is part and parcel of being a Christian. We should be grateful God takes us through this process. However, we should be worried if we are *not* going through this process, as it is part and parcel in our walk with God along the narrow way. This is what God does to his children, He disciplines. If you are not going through struggles, then maybe you are not his child. The other side of the coin is that maybe you are not a threat to the kingdom of darkness, either.

We do not want to hear these things. We prefer not to know that God disciplines His children. We would rather focus upon God's grace that allows us to live as we prefer ~ the "warm fuzzies," in our lives...living our best life now and learning how we can be blessed, prosper, and not worry about accountability. We do not want to hear we must make a sacrifice to serve Jesus, or that there is a high price to pay to be His child. The price could be our very life which we hold dear.

Maybe while reading these words and you have realize you aren't where you need to be. Perhaps you are playing games with God. You may have been running with the world, believing what the world says is truth, and perpetuating the lies. Maybe you have created a god in your own image, who never challenges you and only speaks warm and fuzzy things to your soul? Perhaps you have imagined a god who condones and makes excuses for your sins and gives you a false sense of security that because you prayed a sinner's prayer, you are saved by grace even though you continue to run with and love the world's ways. If so, you are on the broad road, and this is a dangerous place to be. If 83% of people polled will look you in the eye and say they are a Christian, are you one who walks in the truth of what that means?

There is only one way to heaven, and that is through Jesus Christ. The narrow road is difficult, and few find it. True repentance comes when we get a glimpse of our wretchedness, our sinfulness, and our helplessness in the face of a Holy God. We have fear of the Lord, recognizing our need for a Savior and our need for the blood of Jesus to take away our sins, the moment we break and humble ourselves before God. Anything less than an authentically experienced change of heart is not genuine salvation. Even the sinner's prayer, so popular in churches today, is nothing more than words, and empty words cannot save you. Without the heart exchange, without our hearts of stone being replaced by God's heart and Spirit, there is no salvation.

My desire today is not for you to say you know God~ **but for you to recognize whether or not God knows *you*.** Maybe I should not say this, but after the Lord dictated much of the previous message to me, He continued, stating, "*I want you to preach this word. Most will not receive this message, thinking they are just fine, blinded by their true condition, but preach it anyway, that way they will never be able to say they did not know.*"

MY SINCERE PRAYER IS THAT YOU WILL EXAMINE YOUR LIFE IN LIGHT OF SCRIPTURE, THAT YOU WILL CRY OUT TO HIM, RIGHT NOW, COMPLETELY SURRENDERING YOUR LIFE TO THE LORD. PLACE UPON THIS SURRENDER

NO LIMITS OR CONDITIONS. COME TO HIM ON *HIS* TERMS, NOT YOUR OWN, NOR THE WAY YOU HAVE BEEN TAUGHT THROUGH TELEVISION EVANGELISTS OR CHURCHGOING MEN. REPENT FOR TRYING TO CREATE A GOD IN YOUR OWN IMAGE; FALL TO YOUR KNEES BEFORE THE ONE TRUE GOD WHO LOVES YOU.

A special thank you to Paul Washer for giving me the boldness to speak what I have been thinking for years.

Rapture?

Too many are living as if they will be caught in a rapture before the hard times come. They believe that God will take care of everything, so they do not have to prepare for the tribulation to come. The pre-tribulation rapture teaching is accepted as fact in many United States churches, but is not taught in most of the rest of the world. The truth is, no one knows how these end-time events will actually play out.

I would like to share with you what I believe the Lord shared with me several years ago concerning the rapture and the great apostasy (the great falling way). I pray, just like all of you, that it is a pre-tribulation rapture. I do not want tribulation any more than anyone else, of course. The pre-tribulation teaching is prevalent throughout the body of Christ. I always had a check in my spirit when I heard or read these teachings, but I accepted it as truth for a long time, thinking it *had* to be true because most everyone has been teaching it.

Please do not write me back with all the scriptures that seem to support a pre-tribulation rapture. I am aware of them, but truth be told, many seem to require too much reading between the lines to support the hypothesis.

I believe the Lord showed me something, which I would like to share with you. The truth is, as I said, no one knows how the end time events will be fulfilled. We must keep our eyes on the Lord and He will lead us through and safely home.

The pre-tribulation rapture has been used as an excuse, consciously or subconsciously, by the body of Christ to neglect many things God expects us to do. It has made us lazy and apathetic. It has made us silent and complacent, thinking along the lines of *what does it matter, we are going to be out of here anyway?* Therefore being used as a tactic of the enemy.

Many have walked away from God over the past few years due to the difficult circumstances we find ourselves in both economically, and as a nation in general. As for the United States, we have had it very good, for a very long time. God's hand of blessing truly has been on this nation until now. We as individuals are not used to hard times or persecutions here, let alone tribulation and martyrdom as many have endured throughout the centuries.

I believe the Lord showed me that the Great Apostasy, or falling away, referred to in His word will be due to people leaving the faith when the going gets tough as they discover there has not been a pre-tribulation rapture.

We will have to endure tribulation and people will blame God. This is not as far-fetched as one may think. Over the years that I have led Praising in the Park ministry, many have commented that if there is not a pre-tribulation rapture, they will walk away from God because He cannot be trusted.

My response is always the same. It is not God, who cannot be trusted, He is not a man that He should lie. It is man and his teachings that cannot be trusted. In my experience with the Lord, He never does anything the way I expect Him; not how I expect, through whom I expect, or when I expect. Yet it is always perfect. This suggests to me that we just need be ready for whatever comes!

God could remove us before there is any tribulation, which would be nice. He could remove us after the first three and half years, just before he pours out his wrath which would be a blessing, too, or we may be here as the Israelites were, through all the "plagues."

We must not allow the enemy to deceive us. We convince ourselves that it has to be one specific way. The Sadducees and the Pharisees *thought* they knew how Messiah would come, and what He would do, but Jesus did not fit their teachings. However, He *did* fit scripture! The Sadducees and the Pharisees failed! They looked Jesus in the eye. They heard him speak, they saw the miracles, but they did not recognize the God they claimed to serve. They missed their life defining moment.

The truth is, the end time events will not look like we think. It is unlikely they will fit what we have been taught by man, but they will fit scripture. My prayer as you read these words from the heart of the Father, is that you will keep an open mind to hear from Him on this issue, and others.

2007

April 27, 2007

PRAY FOR THE PEOPLE

You did what I asked you to do. You were obedient. The rest is not your concern, but mine. Pray for the people, but mostly pray for the leaders whose hearts are hard and who refuse to hear Me when I call. They are the gate keepers to the souls. The souls respect and revere the man of God, but the man of God is deaf to My call. Pray so all is well with your soul. Grieve not. In My presence you will stand. You heard My call. You responded to My voice and you are My good and faithful servants.

Pray for the people to start hearing from Me directly and not relying on a man to hear My voice. Pray they make Me personal. Pray they bow and humble themselves before Me, for they are in danger, lukewarm and uncaring of the things of God. They blindly continue on their way, believing they are on the right path. Their path leads to destruction. Pray for My people to be saved, truly saved; to hear from My Spirit, to know Me the true and living God and not a figment of their imagination.

Hear and obey Me, My good and faithful servants, for yours is the glory, the honor (not in the world) and the kingdom, for the kingdom of God is at hand. It is closer than you think. Pastors are asleep; too comfortable in their little ivory towers they constructed to keep Me out, and man in. I AM dead to many amidst cascades of chores, rules, and regulations, keeping many from really loving or knowing Me. Pray for My people to humble themselves before the living God; The God of their Fathers, the God of their now, days and tomorrows, the God Who holds their future in My hands. They do not fear Me and they do not desire Me, their only desire is what I can give them.

Forgive them. I have given you a glimpse of My heart's desire to see them step into My plans, purposes I set out before the dawn of time, but they are too busy dancing with the god of this world. They missed a move of God; a call to the people to rise up and be counted for My namesake. Pray for My leaders to honor Me, to seek Me, to seek My face, not business as usual. I rule and reign in the heavenlies. I see all. I know all. Pray for My people to seek the light; to seek My face, while I can still be found, while Holy Spirit speaks.

2008

August 6, 2008

SMALL BEGINNINGS

Mighty men and women of God, gather in one accord for the Lord your God is with you. I have orchestrated this; a small beginning to a mighty outpouring of My spirit. Joshua's, take the land, I am giving it to you to cultivate for My glory, My plans and My purposes. I have spoken, yet so few listen; deaf to My call. But, I have chosen you for such a time as this. The end time harvest awaits. Near and far you will go to accomplish My plans and purposes for this area. The people's eyes and ears will open when they hear My word go forth, not a compromising word but the uncompromising word of God. I will speak in your sleep. You will dream dreams. You will be called to do the difficult things that no one else wants to do, but with that responsibility will come great rewards in Heaven and on Earth.

Do not despise humble beginnings, for I am a God of the harvest. Seeds multiply 100 and 200 fold in My fields; fertile soil. I will bless you with fertile soil, and they will come. The multitudes will come to be healed; to be saved for a mighty outpouring of My spirit. The people will never be the same. The anointing will flow off your lips. When you speak, mountains will move. Out of My spirit breaks forth revival like you have never seen. People will flock to get a word from the man (woman) of God. I will have mercy. I will show grace and lives will change, including yours. Level to level and glory to glory you will move and the people will be amazed at you because of how My power flows through you. Humble servants unite. I have had to clear some plates.

Money will flow into your hands. People can't help but bless you as you move in My Spirit. The good works will multiply, watered by My Spirit, says the Lord. Sometimes you feel alone. People do not understand, but you are not alone. I give you each other, to pray for one another, to cover each other, to love each other and to support each other. Encourage one another for the road is wrought with difficulties and people will come against and accuse. Just know that I am with you, and My plan will be revealed. The spirit is with you. Go with him. Move with him when he moves, be still when he is still. Soak in My presence; remember the more you meet, the more power you will have. Seek My face and be hungry for Me, and I will show you great and mighty things.

2009

2009

God's definition of blessings and prosperity is FAR different then the world's definition. See sermon, titled *Prosperity, Blessing and Favor,* on You Tube. Search under Bear Witness Ministries, (channel; bearwitnessmin). Here is the exact url:

http://www.youtube.com/watch?v=ubjX7o_pKkw&list=UUa 1Y_Uw_pXuSF1D--8q-5Xg&index=8

2009 will be a year of more, more than enough. Disasters loom in the horizon, but I am your God. 2009 is a year of plenty. More than enough for every good work (2 Corinthians 9:8). My people will be blessed. Be encouraged, be of good cheer, for I am Jehovah your God and I am with you. Divisions abound, and will continue, but I am moving in your midst to change the tide of self-destruction to an abundance of blessing. I am Jehovah your God, yet you worry and doubt. Keep your eyes on Me, the God of more than enough. The tide will turn quickly.

They will say it is impossible. Enough is enough, and suddenly change will be upon them. I am a God who speaks in riddles of the night to confound the wise. I speak to the hearts of men. Turn your heart back to Me and I will pour out an abundance of blessing you can't contain. Hide in Me. Fulfill yourselves in Me. Love Me and return your love to Me. The storehouses will be overflowing, as I am a God of abundance, a God of more than enough. Do not be deceived; I did not come to bring unity, but a sword (Matt 10:34). Fathers against mothers, sisters against brothers, and a dad against a child...for I am also a God of justice and not all hear My voice, but you hear Me.

Things are hard right now. Rebellion reigns all around you. Fear not, for I am with you. Fear not, for I am your God and I am with you till the end of this age. Keep your eyes focused upon Me. Let

Me fight the battle. Do you think that I worry? No! I act. I am the author of change and I wish to do a new thing. The past has pressured you. I am a God of the future. Look at Me. New wine is flowing into My children. The old wineskins have been stripped away.

January 21, 2009

CHOOSE

I will baptize you with Holy Spirit and fire. My children, listen to Me, your Father in Heaven. I am your God, and I am faithful. I chose to use you in this end times generation ∼ in spirit and in power. I chose you. You have not chosen yourself, for I ordain the grain, which falls to the ground and dies, to resurrect and produce a harvest beyond imagination, from a tiny seed. I ordain the winds to blow and the days to turn into night. I ordain the true from the false, the wheat from the chaff, and the salt that covers the earth. My people season the earth.

Speak to the darkness and it will flee. Proclaim the light to make the darkness flee from before you. Proclaim the name of Jesus wherever you go, for I am the Alpha and Omega and I chose you as My light, My salt in a dry and thirsty land.

Seek Me in the daylight hours. Seek Me in the darkest of night. Sing to Me, praise Me. Speak to all that that is on your heart and watch Me move among you. Watch Me move in My power and glory. All that you put your hands to, I will bless in this season. I am your God, and I love you. I will bless in ways you never could have imagined. I am a God of blessing.

Look to the small things and see Me move. I am moving in your life all the time. There is not a day that goes by that I do not pour out My blessings upon you. Even in the darkest of nights, even when you feel Me not, even when you think you cannot see Me in your situation, I am there and I am moving. If you settle your spirit before Me, and be still in your situation, you will know that I am God of your days and your nights; the God of every circumstances. I am the God who loves you with an everlasting love, the God who wants to use you more than you want to be used.

Do not fear. Fear not, for I am with you; fear not, for I am your God and I am in your midst. I am in the big and the small, the life and the death. I move amongst you in spirit and in power. Look for Me in every situation, for I am there. I know what you need. I know what you want. I know your secrets. I know your dreams, for I gave them to you. Give your dreams back to Me as a seed this night and watch Me move. Release your dream as a seed back to Me, the One who gave you that dream. I am the dream giver. Open your heart wide to Me, and I will pour out a blessing you cannot contain.

I AM Jehovah your God, look to Me. My people have been fearful. They have looked at the circumstances of My shaking of the economy. They have looked at corrupt politicians and they think I abandoned them, but I am the one doing the shaking. I am trying to get the attention of My people, to wake them up to take their rightful place, and to step into the authority I gave them. I want to move among My people in spirit and in power. Arise O' church; arise and take your rightful place in front of your God!

June 9, 2009

A New Thing That is an Old Thing

I AM the Lord your God and I am in this place. I give guidance. My power and glory reside within you. If you would learn to step into the authority I give you, you would be unstoppable. No demon from hell could stand before you. They will flee, even tremble, as the power of God would be so strong in you. Get a revelation of My presence and power. You carry it with you. Draw from it like a well of living water.

It's time to move forward. There was a time of relatively small growth. It even felt like things were going backwards, but that is about to change. Holy Spirit will do a new thing. Prepare the hearts of My people to receive it. There will be fear as My power descends.

Calm the fear. People will think it is the enemy, but it is Me. I am moving. I desire to do a new thing, which is an old thing, to revive My people. Uncap the wells; dig new wells. I desire to do a new thing, yet it is an old thing to release My power. The Pharisees will try to destroy you the way they tried to destroy My son, but what they thought was the end of Him was only the beginning, as it will be with you. Old things are becoming new!

December 13, 2009

SING PRAISE

Sing praise! Sing praises to the King of Judah. Hear the lion roar as I stir My people to rise up to take this nation for My name sake; to remember My name, to remember My hand of protection, to rise up and speak the name of Jesus, to proclaim My goodness and My sovereignty. I am the Sovereign God. I know what is best. I know which direction this nation should go and it's not time yet. It's not that time for anti-Christ to arise. It is time for My people to arise and call Me blessed; to arise and march to the beat of My drum, to hear the music emanating in My spirit. Let it resonate within you. Proclaim the name of Jesus to the masses.

Rise up sleeping giant and stand before your God. Stand up and be counted. I am asking you, who do you say that I am? Not who do you think I am, not who do you want Me to be...Who do you say that I am? Are you willing to serve Me? Are you willing to go where I tell you to go, to do what I tell you to do? Do you know that faith without works is dead? How could you really know Me, and not obey Me? You couldn't. Obedience is key to your future. The key to fulfilling the plans I have for you. It is the key to spreading the Gospel; the key to knowing the Lord your God. I know the end from the beginning, and I know the direction you are to take. Do not wander alone doing what you think you should be doing; waste of time, waste of effort. Let Me guide you and direct your path. It's the path of least resistance when I lead the way and My angels surround you. I am the tour God of life.

December 30, 2009

2010

I am the Lord you God and behold I am doing a new thing for 2010. I am not finished shaking what needs to be shaken. I am not done changing what needs to be changed. I am the Lord your God who loves you. I am the Lord your God who has your best interest at heart. I know the plans I have for you, says the Lord, plans to prosper you, not to harm you. Do not throw your hands up in disgust and say "what's the use, I have tried everything and nothing seems to be changing." Things need to shake. The shaking is not complete.

Do not become discouraged as the familiar becomes unfamiliar, as things do not look the same, for behold I do a new thing. I will destroy the patterns of the enemy. I will destroy the strongholds of the enemy, and My people will prosper in the wake of the coming destruction. Behold I do a new thing. I love My children too much to leave them where they are, too much, to allow them to continue on the path they are taking. I am bringing My children home. Home to what should be a familiar and comfortable place, in My arms of love, where My grace abounds and overflows into the hearts of My beloved.

It's out of love, I shake. It's out of love, I stir the pot. Behold, I set a table for you in front of your enemies. You will not cower in fear. You will not shrink back. I will vindicate My children and the world will see My hand of favor upon you. My faithful will prosper in the wake of the destruction; transfers of heavenly funds into the hand of My faithful, the ones I can count on to pay it forward, to fund My agenda, to be My hands and feet. Do not fret My loves, your Father is near. You are in the palm of My hand, so fear not... from the heart of the Father.

2010

January 3, 2010

CRUSHED

As the body of Christ was crushed and the blood poured out for your redemption –

As the grapes are crushed to make the wine for the marriage feast –

As the grapes are crushed to make the juice for communion –

The Lord says, hear My voice this day. My people have been crushed under the weight of sin this past year, those things both big and small that have to change before they can move on in Me. Changes need to be made in the lives of all My people. No one is immune from the work I am doing to prepare the body for what is to come. Do not fear. Be of good cheer. Praise in the face of persecution, and you will see Me do great and mighty things in your midst. Do not look back. Look to Me in all things, for I am the God in your midst. Do not look for Me in the old things, look to the future. I am among My people in new and exciting ways in the year 10; a year of multiplied grace.

April 5, 2010

It Is I

Be still and know that I am God. It is I, who holds your future in My hand. It is I who created you, and loves you more than you can comprehend. I am the author and the finisher of your faith. It is I am who loves you. I am everything you will ever need. I am your future. I am your past, washed clean in My blood. I am the supplier. I am the source of all wisdom. I am all you need.

Do not worry about the distractions, those things going on around you; just focus on Me. I am moving in your midst. Your heart grieves for what you see. I am changing that. I am replacing your eyes with mine. I am replacing your ears with mine. I am will anoint your head with the oil of gladness. I am the dream giver. I give, and I help you follow through.

You are not a nobody in My eyes. Today I move in your midst. Today nonsense ends in the lives of My children. Damascus Road, and Isaiah "woe is Me;" a glimpse where disobedience leads. Fear the Lord your God. I will anoint afresh to preach and prophesy. I will anoint once more for wisdom and prosperity. A new dawn emerges; a new day. My angels go out to the north, south, east and west for My glory to reign in your life. A drastic contrast to lifestyles; a drastic contrast of blessings, I will force the hand. I will pull the rug out. Change the season. Speak to the harvest, call it in. Speak to the ungodly agenda, for you have power of counsel and might to bring to pass My agenda. The remnant of America rings out. The Remnant of America prays. The remnant of America rings out. The remnant of America conquers evil. The remnant of America restores My presence among the nation.

June 1, 2010

WHOM WILL YOU SERVE?

Real hope and change only come through the Lord Jesus Christ, not the government. Put your hope in Him, not man.

This is the word I give My servant to speak; Judgment will surely fall against the people of the land, for they have forsaken the Lord God and have chosen to serve other gods of stubble and stone, gods of mammon that neither hear, nor see. Today I say this: the hand of the Lord has risen upon this nation for a season to see whom you will serve; the Lord your God, or the god of mammon. Judgment starts in the house of God.

June 11, 2010

Sermon:

REMNANT AMERICA

Your future is dependent upon whom you choose to honor...America will not unravel because of the Taliban or Al Qaeda. America will not come apart because of abortion or homosexuality. There is one reason America could fail - and that is if America refused to honor the God of this universe. ~ Mike Murdock

There is a story in **1 Kings** where Elijah had just experienced great victory over the prophets of Baal. Then his life was threatened by Jezebel, so he ran off and hid in a cave. God confronted Elijah in his place of hiding and asked, *"What are you doing here?"*

Elijah answered, *"I've been working my heart out for GOD, because the people of Israel have abandoned Your covenant, destroyed Your places of worship, and murdered Your prophets. I'm the only one left, and now they're trying to kill me."*

God responded, *"Go back the way you came through the desert to Damascus...Meanwhile, I'm preserving for myself seven thousand souls: the knees that haven't bowed to the god Baal, the mouths that haven't kissed his image."*

Seems this is similar to the times we are living in. Some of us feel very alone, like Elijah did. We are working our hearts out for the Lord, but it seems like a large portion of the body of Christ is running away; hiding in a cave, afraid. Seems we believe that our very way of life, those things we hold dear, are threatened at every turn. Everything we thought we could count on seems to be shaking. We believe in God, Country, apple pie, baseball and the traditional American way. We believe our Nation was founded on godly values, by godly men and woman; not just prayer warriors...warriors who fought the battle on their knees *and* in the battlefields. They fought for religious freedom. It was the Judeo-Christian values of these men and woman that made this nation great. Everywhere we turn, history is being rewritten to remove our godly heritage. However, it was precisely those values that allowed the Declaration of Independence, Constitution, and Bill of Rights to transcend time. These documents were based on the word and principles of a timeless God; the author and finisher of their faith and ours.

Truth be told, most people don't care about much unless it directly affects them. Apathy is no respecter of age, income or level of education. People don't vote, because they think to themselves, *"What difference will it make?"* We see our government spending trillions of dollars to achieve immediate gratification, unconcerned about what that debt will do to the next generations. People don't care about the quality of their work or appreciate their jobs until they are gone, and teenagers' favorite saying seems to be, *"Whatever."* God hates indifference.

In **Revelation 3:15**, we read,*" you are neither hot or cold; I wish you were one or the other!"* Apathy is rampant, both inside and outside of the church today. The church should *not* be apathetic. God does nothing unless He first tells His prophets; we are the watchmen on the wall, we are to sound the warning. However, because the church read the ending ~ we know how it turns out and that has led to apathy! The church has lost its voice. For the most part, we sat silently while prayer was removed from schools and abortion was legalized as birth control. An entire generation has been killed before drawing their first breath. The mention of God is under attack at every turn.

Increasingly, the remnant of this nation, has developed a fear of man; bullied into silence by political correctness, relativism, finger pointing and threats of a very vocal minority. Our government and leaders, out of one side of their mouths are claiming to stand for the rights of all Americans, not wanting anyone offended. However, they seem to care less when it comes to traditional Judeo-Christian values and the foundation of this nation. It's not just people like Michael Newdow, who sued to have God removed from the pledge of Allegiance, and In God We Trust removed as our national motto. Nor just the American Civil Liberties Union (ACLU) trying to remove every reference of God from our lives...The truth is the media has launched an all-out war on God and Christianity. Think about this for a minute; several polls were conducted throughout America;

1) According to the latest FOX News® poll, 92 percent of Americans say they believe in God, 85 percent in heaven, and 82 percent in miracles. Also, though belief in God has remained at about the same level, belief in the devil has increased slightly over the last few years; from 63 percent in 1997 to 71 percent in 2004.

2) A Newsweek® poll found in 2002 that 87% of respondents favored keeping "under God" in the Pledge. Only 9% were against.

3) In 2003, a Gallup® Poll discovered that 90% of Americans surveyed were in favor of the inscription, "In God We Trust," on U.S. coins. 8% opposed it, and 2% said they didn't know (I don't know about you but it's pretty scary to me that they don't know).

4) A 2004 Newsweek® poll yielded 87% in favor of keeping "under God," with 12% against, and 1% not sure.

5) An online poll launched by MSNBC® in 2005 posed the question, "Should the motto 'In God We Trust' be removed from U.S. currency?" 89% had voted no and 11% had voted yes.

6) Finally, according to a 2008 article from the Washington Post, a *Pew® Poll* in 2008 found that more than half of Americans polled prayed at least once a day.

Isn't it interesting that the media and other special interest groups have made it their business to regularly attack the majority of the people of this nation? Have they not figured out that that 92% of people are the ones who buy the majority of newspapers, watch the majority of the TV, and read the majority of the books? They also compile the majority of voters. I have been self-employed for 23 years; I think biting the hand that feeds you is a pretty foolish marketing strategy. When the nation's media attacks 92% of the market to please 8% it is foolish. This is what I mean by a very vocal minority; they are so loud, and in everyone's face at every turn...it makes these poll numbers seem shocking, as if they should be reversed. **Matthew Chapter 24** tells us, in addition to the scriptures of *wars and rumors of wars, offense* will also mark the last days. **Matthew 24:10** announces, "*And then many will be offended, will betray one another, and will hate one another.*"

In the midst of all this craziness, God has raised up Rupert Murdock, the owner of Fox News®, who is a born again believer. He allows the Name of God to be spoken by Fox News® anchors over the air waves. I guess it's no secret why they are ranked number one, they honor God! The city of Ontario, CA. decided to take a stand last week and they voted and approved their new city seal which states, "In God We Trust." I spoke with the city offices who told me that the majority of the feedback has been positive, with people thanking them for taking a stand.

America's church fell asleep. We became complacent. We forgot that God had something for us to do, and while we were sleeping our unopposed enemy turned the tables, going on the offense and succeeding in gaining a tremendous amount of ground. Truly, the American Remnant is alive and well, and wondering what happened to our freedom of speech. When did everything we believe in, the foundational principles of America and its people, become offensive?

Our remnant honors the founding fathers and brave military men and woman who sacrificed everything to keep us free. They are not ashamed of, and refuse to apologize for, being American. The remnant still believes this is "One Nation Under God," and still proclaims, "In God We Trust. " They who shout, "God Bless America," are alive and well. God wants nothing more than to heal this land, bless the people and turn this national mess around. IF we put Him first, He will respond. We cannot fix this mess on our own, but *God* can! God's Word is full of *If* statements; if we do what He says, we will be blessed, and if we choose not to, we will suffer the consequences. The entire Bible contains stories of men and woman, even entire nations, whose decisions affected outcomes either for good or for bad.

Just like Elijah, who thought he was the only one left, God assured him He had a faithful remnant of those who refused to compromise. **Zechariah 8:12** reports, *For the seed shall be prosperous, The vine shall give its fruit, The ground shall give her increase, And the heavens shall give their dew— I will cause the* **remnant** *of this people To possess all these.* **Romans 11:5** asserts, *Even so then, at this present time there is a* **remnant** *according to the election of grace.* God always has a remnant, and it is time the remnant stands up. We are not called to stand and just confront the darkness; we are the people of God, we should be on the offense, not the defense. There is nothing wrong with us; as a people of God, He lives in us. It is others who have something wrong...they *need* God. The wisdom of God is foolishness to those who are perishing; this fear of man, this need to be politically correct, is not of God. God chose people to be His eyes, His ears, His hands, His feet, and His voice. We are called to speak truth. God is waiting on us. It is time for the remnant to unify, speak up, and be silent no more. It is past time for the sleeping giant, the church, to arise. We need to restore the honor of God to this nation; our fragile lives are in His hands.

A man of God who stood on principle for what was right and was killed for speaking truth once proclaimed, *"I say to you, this morning, that if you have never found something so dear and precious to you that you will die for it, then you aren't fit to live. You may be 38 years old, as I happen to be, and one day, some great opportunity stands before you and calls upon you to stand for some great principle, some great issue, and some great cause. And you refuse to do it because you are afraid. You refuse to do it because you want to live longer. You're afraid that you will lose your job, or you are afraid that you will be criticized or that you will lose your popularity, or you're afraid that somebody will stab or shoot or bomb your house. So you refuse to take a stand. Well, you may go on and live until you are ninety, but you are just as dead at 38 as you would be at ninety. And the cessation of breathing in your life is but the belated announcement of an earlier death of the spirit. You died when you refused to stand up for right. You died when you refused to stand up for truth. You died when you refused to stand up for justice."* ~ Dr. Martin Luther King, Jr. From the sermon "But, If Not," November 5, 1967.

One thing that makes me angry is a Christian who claims they do not have to do anything because God will take care of everything. If you are one of those people, you need to know how *wrong* that line of thinking is. Only 1% of Christians ever share their faith! That is shameful! People are perishing all around us!

Are the prophetic players lining up around the world? Yes! Can we hear the footsteps of Christ coming down the hall? Absolutely! Will the one world government come? Like a steam roller! Will Jesus return for His people? Hallelujah, the sooner the better! But that is not an excuse to be disobedient to what God has called us to do. God made each person special, which is why no one understands your unique gifts and perspectives, because there has never been another one like you before. God gave you distinctive talents that He did not give to anyone else. He conferred upon you an assignment that no one else can do exactly the way you can. God did not choose angels to be His representatives on earth, He chose people. God chose people to appropriate their unique gifts and spread His gospel message. He chose people to be His hands and feet, to demonstrate His love. God chose people to stand up to Pharaoh; He chose people to stand up to the Canaanites, Hittites, Amorites, Perizzites, Hivites, and Jebusites...the Michael Newdows', ACLU, and all the other parasites that would rise against His people. God could choose to put you in any generation in history, but he CHOSE to put you here and now to stand up for Him, to stand up for His principles, to be His voice.

With all that God has done for us, we should be telling everyone who will listen. If God wanted you to brush your hair, would He reach down from heaven and brush it for you? If God wanted you to eat, would He reach down from heaven to spoon feed you? God could choose to part the clouds and preach, He could have chosen angels to do His work, but He didn't, He chose people. God told people to spread the gospel. If you are a people, He means you. If not you, who? Like it or not, excuses or not, God chose people ~ that means you and me!

This is what Remnant America is about. God always has a Remnant ~ His faithful people. It is through that remnant God works. God is calling out, sleeping giant arise and be silent no more, stop being on the defensive and be on the offensive, live lives that lead and do not follow. He desires we take authority in the name of Jesus and stand up for what is right; for truth, justice, and the American way. Stand in the face of accusation and opposition; speak truth, do not fear man. Stand up for God!

Be a part of what of what God is doing. God is asking each one of us, "Who do you say that I am?" Now is not the time to be silent. We need to make a decision to make a difference. We must show the next generation not just what being an American really means, but what it means to be a Christ follower, teaching them about honoring God and country, respecting one another, and voting according to godly values. We need to speak truth, to say what is right and what is wrong. Kids know in their hearts that there *is* a right and a wrong, they just need to hear an adult confirm it. The schools are not going to do it. The media is not going to do it. We have to do it!

How can we as individuals or as a nation be blessed when people who claim to believe in, and live for God are voting people into the highest offices in this land who do not believe God's Word and do not support those things that God holds dear? How can this nation be blessed when leaders are pushing ungodly agendas and, left unchecked and unchallenged, making decisions that are affecting not just this generation, but generations to come? God has been exposing corruption at every level of government and it is shameful, but these corrupt people are not only to blame. How about the people who vote them in and allow them to remain in office year after year, even decade after decade, perpetuating their corruption. Most of the elected officials, as far as I can see, forgot they were elected by the people to serve the people; they have it backwards and now think the people are there to serve them and their every financial whim.

It's time for the excuses to stop, it's time for God's people to be God's people, not just on Sundays in church. We need to be God's workmanship at home, work, school or in the voting booth. It's up to each one of us to stand up and do our part. It's not up to someone else, it is up to us. If not, who? We are the steward. We are the voice. If we don't speak truth, who will? If we remain silent, everything we know, everything we believe in, everything we hold dear will be but a memory and our children, grandchildren and great grandchildren lose out. How will they hear if we won't speak? Faith comes by hearing.

So my prayer is that you will make a decision to be an active part of what God is doing in the heart of people. God is raising up people across this nation and they are finding their voices again. This grassroots movement we have been witnessing IS a move of God.

God wants His people, His remnant, to raise a banner to Him. We are encouraging people to proudly fly the American flag, along with the motto flag, as a sign we are proud to be American and we are not afraid to publicly praise the Lord! The motto is an integral part of the history of this nation. It is our motto, *In God We Trust,* which proudly acknowledges and honors the One true God who has abundantly blessed this nation, that we might be a worldwide blessing. We need to refuse to make excuses or compromise. Let the voices of the remnant crying in the wilderness join together into a mighty chorus that spreads across this nation. Make a statement, choose to be the light, the salt, the love, the Hope, and the voice...be silent no more. Proudly and loudly proclaim **Psalm 26:12** (NLT) *"I have taken a stand, and I will publicly Praise the Lord..."*

Father, help us desire to please You rather than men. Forgive us for seeking, and desiring the approval, praise, and glory from men instead of, and more than, the glory that comes from You. We declare right now that we are free from the praise, criticisms and fear of man. We put our trust in, and put our confidence in, You. We rest safe in Your arms and set on high. We are reassured and encouraged to confidently and boldly say, *"The LORD is my helper; I will not fear. What can man do to me?"* (**Hebrews 13:6**). Just as You sent Jesus, You have sent us into the world to be Your hands and feet, eyes, ears and your heart. You are always with us, and we seek to please You; only You.

Father, in the mighty name of Jesus, we pray for the people of this great nation. We forgive those who have turned their backs on you, on our history, and our heritage. It is our prayer that Your word and Holy Spirit will flow swiftly throughout every city in this country.

Holy Spirit, we thank you for giving us a spirit of counsel, might, and wisdom so that we may communicate a message of hope for this country. You give the wisest answers, and we pray that our words and actions will be a reflection of Your heart and wisdom operating in us, stirring up the hearts and the minds of men, to persuade them that Your will must be done for this nation is to survive as home of the brave, land of the free...In God we Trust, God bless America, and fulfill its destiny. Father, thank You for hearing our prayers and moving Your spirit through this great land. There are earthquakes, famines, floods, economic turmoil, violence, scandals and governmental abuse everywhere we turn. Men's hearts are fainting with fear. May your people recognize the need for a spiritual awakening so this nation will be a shining beacon of light to the world. Forgive us for judging, complaining about and criticizing our leaders when we are called to pray. Forgive us for being silent while You are removed from public life as ungodly agendas are rammed down our throats on every front. Help us to speak truth~ Your Word, to confront the darkness with the light of the word. Cleanse us in Your blood and wash us whiter than snow. Touch our lips with the coals from Your altar as you did Isaiah. Give each of us that same encounter when we come face to face with our true condition in the sight of You, a Holy God. Lord, we desire healing rivers to flow through this nation from coast to coast, overflowing into all nations. We break off this spirit of slumber, this deaf and dumb spirit, and the spirit of witchcraft over the body of Christ. In the mighty Name of Jesus, we pray. Amen.

July 2, 2010

RISE UP

Sing praises! Sing praises to the king of Judah. Hear the lion roar as I stir My people to rise up to take this nation for My namesake; to remember My name, to remember My hand of protection, to rise up and speak the name of Jesus, to proclaim My goodness and My sovereignty. I am the sovereign God. I know what is best. I know which direction this nation should go.

It is not time yet for the anti-Christ to arise. It is time for My people to arise and call Me blessed; to arise and march to the beat of My drum, to hear the music emanating from My Spirit. Let it resonate within you. Proclaim the name of Jesus to the masses. Rise up sleeping giant. Stand before your God. Stand up and be counted.

I am asking, who do you say that I am? Not who do you think that I am, not who do you want Me to be. Who do you say that I am? Are you willing to serve Me? Are you willing to go where I tell you to go; to do what I tell you to do? Do you not know that faith without works is dead? How could you really know Me and not obey Me? You couldn't. Obedience is the key to your future; the key to fulfilling the plans I have for you, the key to spreading the gospel, the key to knowing the Lord, your God.

I see the end from the beginning and know the direction you are to take. Do not wander alone doing what you think you should be doing; waste of time, waste of effort. Let Me guide you and direct your path. It is the path of least resistance when I lead the way and My angels surround you. I AM the tour guide.

October 28, 2010

NOW IS NOT THE TIME

"This is an important word for My children in this hour," your Abba Father.

I am with you. The enemy will not succeed. He is stepping up his attacks in this season to cause people to forget joy. To prevent a celebration of Me. The New Year looms and people's hearts begin to fill with hope for new starts and fresh new beginnings. The enemy wants to destroy that seed of hope that your situation will change. Be alert, do not grow weary and fall into his trap. Though the arrows fly by day, and the darkness looms, look to the light within you to direct your way. When you cannot feel Me, be assured I am still there. When you can't see Me, be assured I am ordering your steps. When you can't hear Me, I am still speaking to your heart. I am the God who said I will never leave you or forsake you. So get up and get on with your assignment and do not let the enemy cause you to doubt or think now is not the time. Now is the time, and you are still the one.

Go into the darkness and shine your light to a lost and hurting world; a witness to My goodness, My grace, and mercy in a dying world. So many looking and searching for more, living in less than My fullness of Spirit. They want more, hunger for more, but they are not being taught more is available; more of My Spirit to fill the void in their lives. I am not holding back, as you empty your heart of things that are not of Me. I will fill it with more of Me.

I am the Lord your God, and I say this is not the time to shrink back. This is not the time to tell yourself, or resign yourself, to living with less than My fullness. This is not the time to resign yourself to live in lack or anything less than My abundance of provision for every good work. Now is not the time to worry and wonder what is coming next. Now is the time for My children to rise up and call themselves blessed, for I am a God of blessing, and I long to bless.

Break off these mind sets the enemy has been placing on you these past few years. Yes, judgments have fallen, exposures have been made, there are great upheavals and fear has gripped the hearts of many, but I am the Lord your God. My children, move through the narrow place and come into the fullness of your inheritance, for I am the Lord your God, and I have spoken.

November 15, 2010

FAITHFUL WITH LITTLE

Because you have been faithful with little, I will trust you with much. I am the Lord your God and I love you. Your future is in My hands. I guide and direct your steps. I choose what I will allow to come into your life, including various tests and trials. The world is fast becoming a dangerous place, but I am still in it and I know My people who have a heart to serve; a people after My own heart. A soft heart; quick to repent when I have been grieved. My Holy Spirit works within a yielded vessel to bring Me glory.

There are wolves in sheep's clothing in and out of the "church," disguised and masked to hide from the one true God, but I see though all. I know the heart of man, and I turn it which way I will. Fear has gripped the nations, but I am still on the throne. I know all things in advance. Tests and trials come along to cause you to seek My face.

Show boats are plenty, but give Me a good solid vessel that is fully yielded to Me, that is My preference. Your future has been written in advance, on the tablet of your heart. I am the author and the finisher of your faith. I have the final say. Your life for My glory, surrendered, is a beautiful thing and made more beautiful with time and your faith. Praise and glory in My house, *that* is what I want. Praise and glory opens doors that have been long shut, breaks the seals of doors in your heart that you did not know were there. I want My people free from bondage. They must have free hearts, and minds yielded to Me!

November 21, 2010

I Am The I Am

I am the Lord your God, King of the Universe, and today I say this:

Look to Me, not man. Stop being distracted by your circumstances. You say you trust Me, but you do not. You are trusting, then looking at your circumstances, then back at Me. You should have your eyes fixed firmly on Me, and then you will not falter. I am the Lord your God, and I know all. I am the I am, and I am in your midst, so why do you worry? Focus on Me, not man, nor your circumstances.

Man says a lot. They say the world will end in 2012. They say I am not real. They say I am made of wood and stone. They say I can't do this or that. They have created a god in their own image. I can't lie. The road is long, and weariness has set in on My people, but you are not alone in this time of trial and testing.

The time has come to bring you into alignment with My plans and purposes; to get in line with the heavenly hosts who are prophesying and cheering you on to run the race. They know what awaits you. You can only imagine. Hear the cheers from heaven. They cover you like a warm blanket to comfort you in your trials.

Never alone, My sights are upon you, upon your heart to change you and mold you into My image. Painful circumstances are to grow you. Do not beleaguer the point by complaining, moaning, groaning and wearing a sad look on your face in public. You are not Pharisees standing on the street corner for show. My joy floods your heart this day, if you receive it. You can reject it. As the rain falls, My Spirit falls to earth to refresh the dry and thirsty land and the dry and thirsty hearts. This is My land. You are My people. Live like it. Laugh like it. Rejoice like it ~ Times of refreshing are here.

November 28, 2010

DUST OFF

I am the Lord your God, King of the Universe. I know all. I see all. The Kingdom of God is at hand. My kingdom invades earth. This next year will be a year of fulfilled prophecy. The words spoken over your life that you have given up on; those words that have collected dust on the shelves of your heart, take them down. Dust them off, look at them. Believe again, My word will be fulfilled.

Discouragement abounds in My church this season, but you are not forgotten. I am the Lord your God; I forget not. Dust off your mind from the disappointment you have felt in this season. The Lord your God is with you. The Lord your God is your strength. The Lord your God is the King of your past, present and future. Have you forgotten I am is I am, and I am is in your midst? I am is in your home. I am is at your work. I am is in your car. I am is in your heart, and I am is alive and well.

Trust Me when all looks bleak. Trust Me when the water rises. Trust Me! When the smoke clears you will still be standing in the palm of My hand. I love you, My child. Each and every one of you, I love. Trust your God. Trust the Lord your God that I know what is best. I know what you need. I know where you are going. You are going with Me. Fear not the rising tide. Fear not the fears of man. You know better. You know I am a God of love, and I love My children, just as you love your children. So why worry? Just trust in the Lord your God. I love you, My child.

December 14, 2010

2011

2011 will be a year of triumph. Not in huge victories, but victory over the little foxes in your life, for it is the little things that stumble you, the little things that distract, the little things that irritate. The little foxes steal, kill and destroy. They dig under the fences. In the cover of darkness, they come. My children have had to be on guard through the day and the night watches. **(Song of Solomon 2:15)** *Catch for us the foxes, the little foxes that ruin the vineyards, our vineyards that are in bloom*). The toll has been high; losses have marked this season. The losses have been immeasurable as this season (2010) shocked the world.

(2011) A season of individual victories and corporate anointing. Move in My Spirit. I ask you this day, do you know Me? Do you know My Spirit? If not, the days ahead will be harder. You will toil and strain in the seasons ahead. My burden is light, My Spirit guides; eases your load. Overcome the foxes, and you overcome your world.

December 15, 2010

PROGRESSIVE VICTORIES

2011 will be a year of progressive victories, not the year of miracles. People are praying, crying out for a miracle that will immediately fix every situation in their life. They are missing Me at work in their lives right now.

It is the little foxes that will be used to turn the tables on your circumstances and deliver you from the wiles of the enemy. (**Judges 15:4-5;**...*so he went out and caught three hundred foxes and tied them tail to tail in pairs. He then fastened a torch to every pair of tails, ⁵ lit the torches and let the foxes loose in the standing grain of the Philistines. He burned up the stocks and standing grain, together with the vineyards and olive groves.*)

I am the Lord your God, and today I say this:

Discouragement has been the word for this past season, but I am at work in your situation to mold you and to change you. I am showing you what is really important in this life, and how to depend on Me solely. Stop striving in your own strength. You are tired, but angel cake is available to you, to strengthen you to run the race.

Call upon the Heavenly hosts. Use the tools at your disposal; be strengthened to run the race. I am the author and finisher of your faith, and there is strength in numbers. You are surrounded by Heavenly hosts. There are more with you than against you. Pray like Elisha did for Gehazi, and your eyes will be opened to see the chariots of fire and the angels with swords in your midst. You fight like the battle belongs to you alone. Have you forgotten every battle fought in Me is victorious? Every battle fought in your own strength fails.

Elisha and the widow; I gave her the gift of a son. Her dream come true, but then the dream died. She did not lose faith. Her dream was brought back to life. Your dreams are not dead, just awaiting resurrection in faith. Will you give up hope by what you have seen in the natural, or stand in faith and see a resurrection and restoration?

Look at the battles of Joshua and the Israelites. What lessons did they learn? What of Gideon? Do it My way and you won't be weary. Stop the grumbling and complaining. *Do everything without grumbling or arguing, so that you may become blameless and pure, "children of God without fault in a warped and crooked generation." Then you will shine among them like stars in the sky;* **Philippians 2:14-15.** Forty years around a mountain is a long time. I blessed them in the desert with water, pheasant, health, clothes and shoes that never wore out; manna from heaven their daily bread of My word, revelation, and provision. They lacked nothing they needed. What they did not have, they did not need.

I am your Heavenly Father, and I know what you need. You need Me! Refocus your attention this season. Complete the transition of man dependency, to God dependent in all things. For Mine is the glory, Amen! I am the Lord your God. Watch and wait for the salvation of the Lord in all your circumstances. The little foxes distract. The little foxes destroy. The little foxes irritate. The little foxes take your mind off Me.

Little Foxes: money, worry, gossip, debt, unforgiveness

December 17, 2010

LOVE

Preach My word far and wide. Preach My word without fear or compromise. Preach My word in love and with joy. Demonstrate My grace. Be mercy. Love. Love is the power that heals hearts and minds. Love the unlovable, because I love them. Love the invisible people, because I love them. Be My hands and feet.

Do you love Me? Do you love Me? Do you love Me? Then tend My sheep. The pasture prepares you to lead. Be mercy. Religion is not merciful, but relationship is. Be merciful toward others and their mistakes. Be mercy. Be gentle with one another's hearts. Stop back biting. Stop doing the enemy's job. You were called to be different. You were called into the light, out of darkness. So leave all the darkness, all that is not of Me, behind.

Look to My light, for in the light is joy unspeakable. In the light is fullness of joy. In the light of My presence is unconditional love; Love that belongs to you. Stop condemning yourself. Stop believing the lies. When I see you, I see My son, white as snow. Stop condemning yourself. You blame yourself for things you cannot control. Accept, but pray over the things you can't change..."BUT GOD," I am a God of "but," and a God of suddenly.

December 18, 2010

FEAR NOT

I am the Lord your God. Your future is bright. You have been discouraged, having not understood the wherefores and why nots. Fear not, for the Lord your God is with you. Fear not, for you have found favor in My sight. The end is not yet; a new beginning awaits, a new beginning in Me. I touch you now this day afresh; awash in My Spirit. I anoint you to pray in My destiny for this valley. Do not worry about those who do not go with you, or what others are doing, or what I have called them to do. You are not alone; never alone. Don't worry about what I want you to do. You are doing it. Rest in My Spirit, allow Me to renew your mind.

December 19, 2010

THE NATION MOANS

I am the Lord your God, King of the Universe, and today I say this; I am the Lord your God. Do not look to another, for I have all the answers. I know your end from your beginning. I know your future. I know your past. I drew you into My arms of love. This nation moans and groans over the events of this past season. This nation moans and groans and needs to come back to Me, and I will heal the land. The President's priorities are all mixed up. Pray for him to turn to God, the one he claims to serve. Pray for the elected officials to seek Me.

December 21, 2010

DO NOT

I am the Lord your God, and I love you. Do not despair. Do not get discouraged for the victory is yours. My children, I will guide and protect you through the storms of life. I will see you safely through to the other side. My word is full of example after example of My intervention in the lives of My people. I rescue, protect, lead and guide, and I do the same for you. You are My child. Do you realize who you are in Me? Triumphant! Victorious! Child of God! Nothing shall by any means harm you. Fear not, for I am the Lord your God. I love you. I am your fore guard and your rear guard. You are surrounded by Me.

December 24, 2010

EARLY "CHURCH"

The early church was full of miracle working power. They were reliant on Holy Spirit. The early church did what Jesus did, just as Jesus did what He saw the Father do. Jesus condemned no one who came to Him. He loved all. He lovingly corrected Peter. He stood firm against the religious folk who condemned the woman caught in adultery; a contrived trial, to which He replied, "Go, and sin no more." His very presence changed the lives of sinners such as Zacchaeus and the woman at the well. He went straight to the root of whatever issue faced Him. He cast out demons and broke bread with sinners. He made them feel worthy; He made the seemingly invisible and unlovable feel worthy.

Love My people; love the invisible, love the unlovable into My kingdom. There are so many lost, angry and hurting people who are waiting for a voice of life to speak to them. You carry the key to life transformation. One life at a time exponentially expands the kingdom. I do not condone sin; be quick to repent to keep the lines of communication clear. The enemy wants nothing more than to convince you that your sin has damaged your relationship with Me, forever. Your sins are forgiven; past, present and future. It is Me who looks at sin through My Son's blood, but the enemy will use your sin to convince you that I no longer love you, that I no longer care, or that our relationship has been forever damaged. Being quick to repent is the same as being quick to forgive; it stops the enemy in his tracks by bringing darkness into the light of My presence.

Forgive yourselves, My children, for I have already forgiven you. In this season, many people are crying out to Me for a miracle. This revelation alone will be the seed of miracles in many lives.

It will turn the tide on your circumstances; it will turn the tide on all those you meet and minister to. Be My Church. Love My people.

December 30, 2010

UNCERTAINTY

I am the Lord your God and today I say this:

I am your strength. I am your strong tower. I am the first and the last and everything in between. Uncertainty has ruled your life. Uncertainty is the name of the game this past season. Can you still trust Me when you don't know what to do or where to go? Can you trust Me with your todays and your tomorrows, even when you can't see the forest for the trees, when all looks bleak and dark? Can you trust Me when every door seems closed, when you don't know where to go, this way or that?

I am still your future and your hope. Trust your King, the Lord your God. The heaviness is lifting off your life. Forgive and forget. You have been angry in this season at your circumstances. The winds of change are blowing. The rain has refreshed the dry and thirsty places of your soul. Your heart is renewed. Those seeds planted in your heart, those dormant seeds, are about to spring to life as a new season emerges; a new season of the soul, a new season in My Spirit, a new season in Me. My words penetrate your heart. I will not let you down. Trust Me.

2011

January 15, 2011

DO NOT FEAR, I AM WITH YOU

Do not fear for I am with you. Do not fear, for I am your God. What befalls the people will devastate the hearts and the minds of all those who are not firmly planted on the rock of salvation. The fence is full of people balancing, walking, and talking. Soon many will lose their balance, forced to take to a side; Me or the world. The world laughs at the notion of the one true God; a sovereign God, a holy God, Maker of heaven and earth, but the day of reckoning is fast approaching, for the world will see Me in all My power and glory, as the heavens shake and the earth splits.

My glory comes in like a flood, putting fear in the hearts of men. Fear of the one true God is healthy. It is missing in My church today. I am not in My rightful place. Man has made Me in his own image. Man will get a glimpse of a Holy God and see himself in comparison; he will be found wanting. Dark days are coming upon My church and My nation. The darkness is the absence of My light, but My light will shine more brightly through the dark night of the soul. I have made a way of escape for My children. Abide in Me. Abide in My presence. Read My word, fill full of Holy Spirit. Listen for My instructions through the dark days. I will guide you, lead you, and instruct you in My ways.

Fear not, for I am with you. Fear not, for I am your God. The remnant of My people are safe in My arms; you are covered in My wings. The glory surrounds you, move in it. You are surrounded in it. It is your light in the dark; My power to accomplish My plans and purposes through you in the earth. You are not lost as the world is lost. You are not found wanting. You are My sons and daughters, and I make a way of escape for you. My presence is your escape. You have been given eyes to see and ears to hear in a deaf and blind world. Follow My footsteps. Walk in My glory cloud. Move when I move, and stop when I stop.

Feed the hungry, heal the sick, cleanse the lepers, cast out demons of doubt and torment; deceiving, familiar spirits. My church is divided. My people faint out of fear of calamity coming upon the world. Be salt and light. Lead the way through the darkness. As the plague of darkness fell on Egypt, My people could see in the dark and they were unaffected. They could see as if it were light. That is how it will be for you, if you remain in Me.

January 20, 2011

GRACE IN THE MIDST OF CHAOS

The taunts, the jeers that have you so discouraged are but for a fleeting time, then you will enter a time of rest in Me. Protection surrounded by My arms of love and grace, and you will have it easier for a time; A season of grace in the midst of chaos. In Me, you will move following the pillar of fire. You will speak with voices of angels, with the power and authority of My kingdom representatives. You will have what you say, so be careful what you speak into existence.

Pray! Pray for the fire of God to come upon you, to burn up your flesh and your fleshly desires, so all that is left is a sweet savor unto your God. When the smoke clears you will be standing stronger than before, surrounded by My glory.

The taunting and jeering has polluted your hearts and minds, but I am God. Renew your hearts and minds. Wash them in My word. Praise and worship Me to perfect the changes I have begun in you. You are not what they say you are. You are what I say you are, and that is My child. You are My covenant being, made in My image, created for My glory, fashioned to speak My words, to sing My praises; created to bring Me glory, in season and out.

Just believe! Just believe I have your best interests at heart. My word speaks of My love for you. If you do the "if's," I will do the "thens." I want to pour out the "thens" to perfect and to bless a mighty nation. Put away the lies, the deceit spoken by the enemy to distract and to move My people out of faith and that place of blessing, for I am the God of more than enough, a God of abundance. I hear the sound of an abundance of rain for those who stand in faith, have stood in faith, refusing to believe the lies, and have not been shaken; those whose foundations are still standing as the spirit earthquake spreads across this nation. Grasp what it means to be My child! You are loved and adored, all that I have is yours!

February 1, 2011

This Land

My child, the enemy of your soul is working overtime to cause you to doubt your calling, to cause you to doubt My endless love for you. He wants you silent. He wants you contained in a box of the mind; out of faith and in doubt of My love and My glory at work in the lives of My people in the world. Where doubt rules and reigns, there is no place for Me to move and breathe and have My being. Serve Me wholeheartedly with abandon, for My plans and purposes, not man's.

Truly worship Me in spirit and in truth. My glory flows down from heavenly places into the heart of man. That pillar of fire and cloud of glory the Israelites followed is now living inside of you, giving you guidance and direction. Follow your guide through the desert places, across the Jordan into the Promised Land; the land of milk and honey, the land of blessing, the land of your fathers. The land flowing with milk and honey is still available to My people.

This land is that land. My people, turn back, and I will heal the land. Stand for Me, and I will bring you into that place of blessing. You are not a grasshopper. You are a warrior of King Jesus. I led Joshua, but he still had to fight the enemies in the land to gain his inheritance, and so do you. So rise up and fight, My child. Rise up and fight. I am the brass ring. I am the prize. My kingdom plans depend on you doing your part in the earth and in the Spirit. Don't give up, press on. Press on My child. You've already won. You have the victory. It's your enemy that hasn't figured that out yet. They are still fighting, but they have no victory against My strong right hand, for that is where you sit; in the palm of My right hand.

Just follow My lead. Follow My instructions. As long as the Israelites were obedient, they won every battle. Your enemy refuses to throw in the towel until the final round, always believing he can get you off track. Distractions, distractions, distractions reign in the kingdom of darkness. You live in the light. Follow the light of My glory, which emanates from your heart.

February 8, 2011

Vision:

CRUISE SHIP

All of the people on earth were evacuated to a cruise ship (think Noah's Ark); there was no choice to be made, whether you believed that the end of the world as we know it, or not was coming. The chaos that was in the earth; disasters, crime and disease, the birth pangs of the last days, had risen to flood proportions.

We were on the ship called Holy Spirit, by God's grace. Everyone was assigned a number. We were being protected for a time from the wrath that had fallen on the earth. As in the days of Noah, the people ate, drank and were merry and had no idea or care for what was going on around them.

I am not sure how long we were on the ship, but suddenly, over the loud speakers, came repeated alarms, followed by warnings; "Everyone go to your seat. Go find your seat." Some people were just walking around, oblivious to the warnings. They could care less. Others were rushing around trying to find their seats. There were workers on board (Angels) who were hurriedly trying to help people find their seats. The urgency was overwhelming!

There was a huge amphitheater with pie shaped sections of seats. The seats looked like theater seats with burgundy velvet upholstery; the kind where you have to push the seat down to sit. On the end of each seat bottom was a number. As I watched, some of the pie shaped sections filled up. People were laughing, talking, and oblivious as huge walls slid down on all sides of a section once it filled. The section was then moved out of the auditorium. The occupants' eternal destinations sealed.

I ran down the back aisle and saw my daughter with my grandsons. She had already found her seat, but was looking for me. I asked where one of my grandsons was and she pointed at the stroller next to her. I picked up my other grandson to help her since she was alone with the two kids. The worker (Angel) told me that we needed to find my seat. Still carrying my grandson, I ran, following this worker. We arrived at my section. There was hardly anyone sitting there yet. The angel walked down an aisle and pushed the seat bottom down checking the number. On the back of each seat was a mark. Mine said "going." I looked up to the Lord and said "Thank you," as I touched the mark.

When I turned around; one of my son's was behind me. The angel told him that they needed to find his seat as well. We all ran to look for his seat. The angel pushed a seat down for him; the mark read "not going." My son told the angel, "NO, that is not My seat." The angel checked the number and apologized, then pushed the cushion down on an adjacent seat which was marked, "going." He sat and I ran back to my seat.

I believe this vision indicates that God has extended his grace on the world. He is holding back the full wrath of the enemy/His judgment, but the time of grace is nearing its end. We are being warned to "find our seat," to make a decision which way we will choose; to go with God, or remain on our journey without Him. There was an incredible urgency ~ a heaviness and burden I felt, and continue to feel.

God, in His great mercy, is giving us yet another warning! We all have unsaved family and friends. What are you doing to reach them? What about you today? What does your seat say?

When the door slams shut, what will your eternal destiny be? Separated from God, or moving into His open arms of love?

February 11, 2011

WOLF IN SHEEP'S CLOTHING

I am the Lord your God and the nations are trembling at My feet, for the earth is My foot stool. Bring Me praise and glory from the heights of heaven to the lowest valley, for the dawn of a new day awaits those whose focus is on Me. The enemy is infiltrating; a cunning fox, a wolf, disguised in sheep's clothing. He thinks he is going to win the game of life, but I am about to expose a plot. Scheming, he has been bragging about getting away with the biggest scheme yet, but the disguise is about to come off.

As with Little Red Riding Hood, grandma is not who she says she is. She is a wolf in sheep's clothing. I am about to rip off the disguise and show the world the wolf, who is not who he says he is, Muslims infiltrating the highest offices in the land, pulling the wool over the eyes of the people.

Expose, I tell you, expose. I must to protect My remnant from a government gone wild with arrogance and power. Ignoring Me, they charge ahead with the agenda of distraction, listening to a man of means and power bribing them, rather than turning to the God of power. Dirty money is used to destroy, rather than to build; money with a demonic agenda is paying off news outlets to lie and ignore, rather than tell the truth and expose. Asleep at the wheel.

Those who do see, silenced and minimized. It is about to blow up in their faces. Asleep on the job, they see no evil, hear no evil, and speak no evil. Sins of omission are still sins. Your God is still on the throne, and I hear the cries of My remnant.

February 15, 2011

NOT ALONE

I am the Lord your God. I am the King of the Universe; today, I say this:

You are My chosen people, flesh of My flesh and bone of My bone (refer to Jesus walking the earth); My Spirit lives within you. You live and breathe and have your being, fulfilling My plans and purposes within the earth.

You are not alone! So many of My children feel alone, afraid, not knowing which way to go; this way or that, but I assure you, in voice, and in being, as My word says, you are not alone. I will never leave you nor forsake you, My beautiful, loving children. Though darkness will rise like a flood, and fear will grip mankind...though fear may grasp the heart of man, My children will remain strong. Our bond is that of a threefold cord, not easily broken.

My covenant people, I am your God and you are My children. Settle the issue in your hearts. Bring your fears to Me, the dream giver, and move forward anew and afresh. Your dreams did not die permanently. They died for a time and season, to prepare you for the realities of your dream. It's not all glamorous; there is much hard work. If I did not prepare you, you would not be able to handle, nor stand under the anointing. Fear not for lack of My presence; when I am silent, I am still with you. My still small voice is there, whispering quietly to help you settle your spirit before Me, learning to hear from Me in a new, more intimate way. I want you desperate for Me, for My presence. I want you to miss Me and seek Me, heart, mind and soul when you think I am gone; rest assured, My precious child, I am always with you.

Open your hearts wider and let more of the King of Glory come in. Too many closed minds, hearts and bodies in this season. Open the door. Do you hear Me knocking? Open the door of your heart, once again, to new levels of glory and anointing. I AM the same God. I change not. It is the seasons that change to grow you.

Praise Me, My child. Praise Me in the midst of the storm. Dance with Me as David danced. His heart was after mine. He did not care what others thought of him. He danced the victory dance and he was unafraid to cry tears; brokenhearted, and feeling alone, when he did not understand the desert place. He did not understand that the battles and the desert were preparing him to reign as King.

You don't understand that every battle you face and walk through in Me makes you stronger. It prepares you for the next position. Each battle will be harder than the last. The enemies are stronger, BUT SO ARE YOU! Stand before your enemy as David did, speaking *"How dare you mock the name of the Lord and His anointed!"* (**1 Samuel 26:9**) for you are anointed, each and every one of you, for such a time as this. Where there is darkness, My light shines much brighter. Though you may be mocked, and the enemy engages you in battle, raise the sword of My Spirit. My word will strengthen you. Be doers of My word. Holy Spirit will help you see it through to fruition.

It doesn't matter what it looks like. David did not understand why he was told he would be King of Israel, then run into the desert, hiding in caves, fighting hunger and the enemy. Like David, you are surrounded by mighty men and woman of valor who support you and stand with you, believing, for they know your future depends on them, and their future depends on you succeeding.

I am proud; a proud Father when I see My children. My family, come together in unity. You need each other! Come together church...not "churches," *the* Church, the body of Christ. You have divided yourselves, hidden behind walls of separation and denomination, but I call you out. This is not what I intended. The church formed in the day of Jesus would have no idea what you are talking about when you speak your idea of "church." Man made plans, programs, and just so many songs. Every week the same; no room for the God you claim to worship. What's it going to be; Man's way, or My way? God's way? Am I not the God you claim to serve? When did My word become optional? My word is My Son, and if you reject My word and do not live by it, you do not live in Christ.

Think about what you are hearing in your church; more importantly, what you are not hearing. Is the Helper welcome in your church, or is man in charge? Be dependent on the Helper. Know the Helper intimately. If your church is not controlled by the Helper, but by programs and things of man, beware...your eternal destination may depend on information you are missing. Your plans and purposes set out before time depend on the leading of the Helper. Navigation through dark seasons of the soul depends on the helper. My heart grieves. The Helper has been rejected by much of the body of Christ. Do you want to know why you lack power, why you are not healed, why your prayers do not avail much? It is simple, you have rejected My Helper. I want to do a new thing, which is an old thing. I long to restore My original intents and purposes for My church, to build it upon the rock of salvation; My Son, Jesus the Christ. Restore the Word of God. Restore My Helper.

A word of warning to My people; My church needs to be "The Church," and the church can't be "The Church," as it was in the days of Paul, Peter and John, without change back to My original intents and purposes. Embrace My Helper. He is not optional.

He is your strength and your guide; your road map to the future. His directions can save your life or change your situation. One word can forever change your destiny. It can show you how to win a battle, to speak a word that can forever alter a life, or lead you to that person to bless or be blessed. A missed or obeyed instruction alters lives; a direction, a moment in time, a destiny. One word can pluck a life out of the hands of the enemy and set a soul on the path of righteousness. Be sensitive to My spirit, the Helper. Seek Him as you seek Me. Seek Him as you seek My Son, for We, three, are One.

It's out of love that I speak these words to My church. My children, pay attention to My calling; so many are living in compromise, so many don't even know what My will is for them as a member of the body of Christ. Turn back, turn to Me, the Lord, your God. Refuse to compromise for My namesake, refuse to put emotions before Me, refuse the things the enemy puts before you that I abhor. Compromise has invaded My church. From all sides, the enemy has advanced, even though the fortresses you call your churches. Men have embraced, if not encouraged, compromise. Some things are just not negotiable. Why do you tolerate sin in your midst as if it was Holy? Love the sinner, not the sin. Embrace the sinner, do not condone the sin. Sexual sin is tolerated and rampant; sorcery and drugs are tolerated.

You are supposed to be changing lives; a mighty force for the world to reckon with, a mighty force of My power and glory for the world to wonder. Instead, you have allowed the world to change you. In the name of tolerance, the stench of sin rises up before me to epic proportions within the church. It is expected in the world and tolerated in church. It is out of an abundance of love that I warn *this* church, *you will stand or fall based upon what you tolerate.*

I am a loving and patient God, but I will not be mocked. Throw away your agenda and throw away these plans of man. Throw away the programs to build the church. I am the God who builds My Church when that church is built upon Me. Don't let numbers fool you. I am not in many big churches, I have not been invited. I have been replaced by man's desire to tickle ears, rather than grow in My word and in the power of Holy Spirit. I often wonder, are you praying to the sovereign, Holy God, or to a god made in the image of man? You don't honor each other, how can you honor Me? Has the cross lost its meaning in a time of grace? I never intended for sin to abound in My Church, that grace would abound much more. *My* church was to use the power of Holy Spirit to change the world, not to let the world change it.

Pastors, if you love Me, feed My sheep. Don't compromise the Word of God, though it is popular to do so. Change the world; don't let the world change you. Return to your first love. Move out of the walls. Be "The church" in the community; be the church to the hurting, broken, and hungry. Move out of your realm, the little worlds you have created where you are comfortable, where everything, and everyone, has a place...everything in its place. Move out of your comfort zone and embrace the world I have created. Live the love of Christ. When darkness comes, people will ask, "How do you do it? How do you still stand?" Tell them it is not you who is standing, it is the God in you who stands!

February 21, 2011

ENCOURAGEMENT

I have been giving you much encouragement lately through My other children, to build you up and give you the confidence you need to step out and let Me move through you. Change is coming in your midst and ministry. You will minister My presence in Spirit and in truth. You will do it in My love and strength, and people will be blessed. My heart for My people will be revealed in the way you minister, in the way you handle yourself. People believe you care, and you do care. You want what I want, My very best for them in all things. So many hurt and broken people, so many hurting hearts and destroyed lives; they need Me! The enemy has had his way on the hearts and the minds of so many of My children who don't fully realize that their strength, their protection and grace only come through Me.

Striving to gain riches all the world says is important, I have exposed the true motivation in the lives of My people, the people I call Mine, My namesake. Those who do not choose to go deeper will have a harder time with the changes happening upon the earth.

I am the Lord your God, King of the Universe. I hold each planet in the palm of My hand, all at the same time. I am a big God, far bigger than your problems, for I am the author and the finisher of your faith. I know the end from the beginning, and I tell you the end is not yet. Eyes are looking up at Me in expectation of My coming, and that is good, but I call My people to turn their eyes upon their fellow man and see them, hurting and lost. I challenge you to step out of yourselves and comfort, thinking, "I am safe," and that is all that matters.

There are people you know, and brothers and sisters you don't know, who are praying for those you meet; those who cross your path. They are praying for their salvation, just as you are praying for the salvation of friends and loved ones who cross their path. The unsaved cross the path of one of My children daily.

Speak. Speak into the lives of these people. They may not listen to their loved one praying, but they may listen to you. There is less pressure when a stranger plants seeds of My kingdom; it allows time for Holy Spirit to work. Remember when you were a teenager and you did not want to listen to your family, but you asked advice from an adult you trusted, and then you thought about it, and you made that advice your own thoughts? It's the same in the kingdom. You plant and I make it grow.

Stop the fear mongering. If you are firmly planted on the rock, you have nothing to fear as the wars and rumors of wars rage, as the birth pangs continue to escalate. All those words I gave you previously for My people said you have nothing to fear, but the world will faint in fear. I have said and done all of this shaking to realign your priorities and get you fully focused on Me. You have had to learn to trust Me in all things, as the rug was pulled out from underneath your feet. The rock did not shake, just your wrong thoughts and desires as I realigned your mindsets to prepare you for what lies ahead. You must trust Me in all things, even when you don't know the way, or the path you were following suddenly disappears.

Look for My provision in ALL things and you will find it. Trust not your own understanding. You are safe in My arms of love. Some will go home and others will remain to usher in these last days, but either way, if you are in Me, you are safe. That has not changed. The light in the darkness will shine bright and clear, there will be a sharp demarcation. The heart of man will wax increasingly evil, but the heart of My children will remain soft and pliable through it all, come what may. I will provide for My people with ravens as I did for Elijah; with cruses (jars) of oil that will never run dry, with jars of flour that refill nightly, with multiplication of fish and loaves. It is all in My word to show you I can provide an abundance, from little, for My children. From a small seed proceeds a mighty oak, from a small jar can come an endless supply.

I am more concerned that you focus on loving one another, and those you meet, into the kingdom. Many will be running scared, not knowing what to do, or where to turn. You will be their light in the darkness; a light that points the way to Me. It is Me, in you, that will light their path to come to Me, heart, mind and soul. Your confidence in Me will be attractive to those in fear. They will want what you have, and that is Me. In contrast to the world, you will be firmly planted by the streams of living water. A sturdy, solid oak standing tall, unmoved by the circumstances of the world as long as you abide in Me.

February 23, 2011

EYES OF ETERNITY

I am the Lord your God, Master of all. Turn your attention to Me and ignore the distractions. Distractions equal destruction. What you take so seriously is nothing but a game of cat and mouse, a game of the enemy, like a child trying to do this and do that to get negative attention. All the while, the enemy is laughing at you. When you turn your focus onto them, they just laugh because you fell for their scheme.

You cry, weep, moan, groan, murmur, and complain. You act devastated, and you do not even realize they are laughing at you. It's comedy central. See your problems, test your problems with eyes of eternity, put things in their proper spiritual perspective. Will it really matter a day, a week, a month from now? What about five or ten years from now? Can you control it? Yes, or no?

Do your part, I will do mine; faithful to the end, to see you through every situation without fail. I, the Lord your God, am bigger than your problems, bigger than anything you face, bigger than anything the enemy throws your way. My child, My love, know who you are in Me. I speak plain; no gimmicks, no games. Know who you are in Me; Victorious warrior child, walking, speaking, moving in My authority. When you speak, it's as if I spoke. Do not let the enemy steal your blessing, your joy, or your authority in any situation in life. My children, KNOW WHO YOU ARE IN ME.

March 2, 2011

I Love You Too Much

I am the Lord your God. How I love My children! I am not angry or distant. I am your loving Abba, Father. I care about every want, and need in your life. I want the best for My children; not by the world's standards, but by My kingdom standards, higher than the world's standards.

I love you too much to allow you to continue in your sins. I love you too much to allow you to trust in anyone but Me. I love you too much to allow you to remain in wrong mindsets. Kingdom mindsets, that is what I am calling you to; kingdom mindsets, kingdom focused lives, kingdom focused living. In the days ahead you must come away from a government focused mindset to focus on the King. Not just the king of this nation, or the king of the world, but the king of the universe. All that is known and unknown to you, I am the Master of all. If I can support the vast expanse of the Heavens, I can meet your needs. Trust in Me, My child. All is well.

March 4, 2011

WOUNDED WARRIORS

I love you My child, with an everlasting love; a love you can know nothing about in its fullness until you stand in My presence. How deep? How far? How wide are My arms of love? You cannot fathom the extent of My love for you. It is from everlasting to everlasting.

I set eternity in your hearts; an eternity with Me, in My arms of love. Each and every one of you is invaluable to My kingdom purpose. Each and every one of you has been given a circle of influence, lives to change. How will they know if you don't speak? How will they know of My love? How will they know of Me? Hurting hearts, minds and souls ache for Me. Wounded, dead people, going through the motions of life like zombies, never getting to the point; it's about Me.

Tell them I love them. Striving for things of the world won't, and isn't making them happy. They are even more miserable then they were before the bondage. There are wounded warriors of the faith as well. So many stifled and broken hearts, wounded by religion; by those Pharisee hearts; the Jezebels and Ahab's, the Saul's, chosen to raise up My children, only to destroy their hearts out of jealously. They sought to kill dreams, visions, gifts and anointing of My precious children. Out of control Jezebels seek to destroy the joy and faith of My children; they incur bondage and control. Break free! You are free. Fear no man.

March 5, 2011

MEN

Men, I am calling you into account this day. Many of you have left wives and children to fend for themselves, that you may fulfill your selfish needs and agendas. Many of you verbally and emotionally abuse your wives, not honoring the weaker vessel, not honoring them the way I honor them...as if I can't see. You have sought and succeeded in opposing My children in the name of inferiority, in My name. I made you equal, man and woman. Have you not read, there is no male or female in the kingdom.

Husbands, have you not read you will be called into account for every word that proceeds from your mouth? Do you not realize that when you talk to your wife, you are talking to Me? Husbands, you have not stood when you needed to stand, spoken when you needed to speak, and protected your family when you needed to protect them. Society is in disarray; not because of homosexuality, pornography, or the government, but because of men who have failed to allow Me to be the Lord of their lives. Men, you must allow Me to live through you, to be the leaders I have called you to be; to love, protect and care for your family, forsaking all others but Me.

Get in order, heads of households. A day of reckoning is coming, and it is you I will call into account for every abusive word, for every time you were to stand in the gap for your family and failed, for not loving your wife like I love the church, for not loving your own wife and children like you love your own body.

Families are floundering. Your kids have no godly example and are following the world. The rise in homosexuality and other sins; drugs, alcoholism, porn and the perpetuation of abuse ~ all addictive behaviors ~ are because the needs of children are not

113

being met in their homes. Society is given over to the wolves in sheep's clothing, for the protector is too busy in the world. Stop here and now the blame game. No, it's not your wife, it's not your kids, it's your failure to lead I am looking at right now. You have handed your authority and your God given power over to the enemy without a thought, or concern, for the mammoth repercussions of your actions. It has come up before Me a vile stench. Make it right. Ask Me with a humble heart, and I will set things straight. Be who you were called to be in Me. Love like you were called to love your family. Forsake your selfish desires. You have no one to blame but yourselves for handing over your God given authority to the enemy by failing to stand in the gap; failing to pray, failing to speak blessings over your family, and children, going your own way. You have gone the way of the world instead of My way; the narrow path. All of society suffers. Men of God, rise up! On your knees, prostrate yourselves, humble your selves under My mighty hand to get yourselves in position to reach your family and take back all the enemy has stolen. This is your battle in Me.

Dream:

A WARNING TO WORSHIP LEADERS

I had a dream that I believe is a warning. It was aimed at all, but particularly worship leaders.

The gist of the dream is a warning; the new age and occult is in the church and many who love the Lord will be, and are being misled. This is for actual church services as well as "soaking" CD's. There is also a warning in the dream against profiteers. This is verified I believe as a few weeks ago I saw a YouTube video of a well-known TV pastor pushing RAVE music as a way to go "deeper" in the Lord!

In this dream, I was invited to attend a worship conference. I arrived early. A friend and I entered a side room to wait. A woman came into the room in nurses scrubs (speaks of a healing environment) and she began to yell at me and accuse me of all sorts of things. I replied that I had only arrived a few minutes prior, but she continued to yell. I repeated that I had just arrived a few minutes before, and she finally left. She did not want me to see what was going on.

I then walked into the room where the conference was to be held and saw worship leaders from various churches. They were all drumming together in an occult drum circle. On the walls were several of the "In God we Trust" flags we offer through the website *RemnantAmerica.com*. There were also other Christian banners.

When they saw me they stopped drumming, stood, and hid their drums. They began to set up for a more "traditional" worship setting. I turned to leave, but then decided to watch and see what would happen.

115

I saw worship leaders whom I know, ones who seemingly love the Lord and I thought to be full of the spirit, come into the room and get their instruments out. Others came in and began taking drums out of their boxes, setting them up to continue the occult drumming. At that point, I decided it was time to go. I had seen enough. I walked out to the lobby, where I observed people selling T-shirts. Grieved for God, I left.

Instead of worship and praise being lifted up for no other reason than to glorify God, there was compromise with the world, which included the new age/Occult movement. The merchandising had the feel of the money changers. God was being used as a marketing tool; the people were focused upon profiting from something that should have been heartfelt worship directed to the Lord. Many of our churches come across this way today...using events and activities for merchandising in addition to glorifying their "music" or traditions of men.

March 9, 2011

Dream

STONES

I had a dream last night. I was in a neighborhood with large two story homes. There were two homes right next to each other. The first was an attractive, tan stucco, with a manicured lawn The other was gray, and apparently still under some construction, as indicated by a yard in disarray and work trucks still parked.

I was standing in front of the gray house. There was a large delivery truck in the yard. Two people on the roof of the house started to throw stones at me. They then jumped from the roof onto the top of the truck, continuing to throw the stones.

I looked around and saw lots of stones on the ground. I picked up a handful and threw them into the air. Immediately, dark clouds began to move in; storm clouds. I threw more stones into the air; boom, earth shaking thunder followed. As I threw more stones into the air, more thunder ensued. The two people on top of the truck became frightened. I awoke.

This dream served as a reminder that, when under attack or persecution, our weapons are not carnal. **2 Corinthians 3-4** clearly states *³For though we walk in the flesh, we do not war according to the flesh. ⁴For the weapons of our warfare are not carnal but mighty in God for pulling down strongholds.*

March 11, 2011

INVITE ME

I love you, My child. How many years did you spend looking for love in all the wrong places? You looked for it in substances, but you did not find Me. You looked for My love in other people, but you did not find Me, because they were as empty as you and looking for love in all the wrong places too.

A glimpse of My love is a weighty responsibility; a testimony to be shared with others. A glimpse of the Holy One is a life changing encounter, not to be taken lightly. A glimpse of My love is a glimpse of My grace in the lives of My children. A glimpse of the power of change in lives, in hearts, and in minds. I am the Lord your God. I give you My strength to fight every battle, to stand in the face of adversity. You can do it all in Me or you can choose to fight in your own strength...but, why? I offer you mine.

Invite Me in. So many people and places where I am not welcome; invite Me into your circumstances. Complaining is not the same as a prayer or an invitation. The people of Japan were going about the business as usual today when disaster hit. This is why it is so important to keep your eyes on Me. Invite Me into your day, as you never know what disaster may befall you. An acute ear to hear My instructions can be the difference between life and death, blessing or cursing. Invite Me to weddings and games. Invite me into the car on the drive home. Invite Me into the big and the small things in your life. I will not intervene where I have not been invited. Pray Me into every situation and watch the tide turn. Now that you have found Me, do not limit where you allow Me to join you.

Cling! Cling to Me in the face of adversity, in the face of uncertainty, for I am. I am a certain God. I am the God of the harvest and some of you feel you have been sowing and sowing, and have little to show for it. Every effort you make to further My kingdom will be multiplied back to you in this life, and applied to your heavenly account. Nothing you do for Me goes unnoticed in Heavenly places.

March 14, 2011

LIGHT THE WAY HOME

I am the Lord your God, and today I say this:

I am your king. I am your first love. Do not deviate from Me. There is protection under My wings for My people. The dangers are increasing but so is My presence in the lives of My people; tangible, touchable, you will feel My presence in ways you have only imagined. In the days and weeks ahead, I will be with you, to lead you in all truth. I will give a fresh release of My Spirit into your hearts and minds; a flood of emotions, full of love, safety, and security in an uncertain world. A place in My presence where neither moths nor rust can destroy. A place prepared just for you.

You live in My heart. My beloved child, you are an extension of Myself into a cold dark world, you light up the night in ways you never could dream. My presence is increasing, not decreasing as so many are saying. My presence is increasing in the lives of individuals.

Revival starts with one spark igniting a fire of My Spirit that no man can extinguish, for I am the Lord your God and I will never leave nor forsake My beloved children. You can't imagine what darkness may befall the earth, but I already know what is to come; Stay focused on Me and know that all is well. There is protection under My wings, glory on the horizon, and a new release of My power in unprecedented ways.

Even the early church will pale in comparison to this move of God. They were few; you are a multiplied many, and My glory will cover the earth. When the spark ignites, the flame will not be extinguished in the hearts and lives of My children until I return for My people. Unprecedented, unprecedented, unprecedented; get ready, prepare yourself, consecrate yourself afresh and anew to be the embodiment of My Spirit upon the earth. Holy, empty vessels, to be filled with My presence. Holy, empty vessels to receive My glory. Holy, empty vessels, will move in My Spirit to reach the lost and prepare the way of the Lord. My people have felt like John the Baptist crying out in the wilderness, *"Prepare ye the way of the Lord."*

People will begin to seek YOU in the desert place, seeking the river of the living water that flows without end through you. They will never thirst again. A people sent out to do a new thing, which is an old thing, for the old things have passed away and will be given new life; resurrection power to alter the face of humanity...a power so great, people will faint out of fear. Signs and wonders will once again follow My people on the highways and byways; a force of change in the world. The light of My love, the light of My presence will not be snuffed out. It will not be extinguished, to the contrary; a light to nations, to light the way home. My children, I light your way home

To clarify, I believe this next "revival" will be individuals, reaching individuals in the midst of great darkness and persecution as it was in Jesus' day.

March 16, 2011

Judgment Starts In The House of God

Pastors, stop sacrificing your own sheep to the god of this world. Those sheep I sent you to love and lead, you are sacrificing upon the altar to Jezebel; the altar of control, at the sake of love. Where is the love, the love for My children, the children of My own heart?

Instead, programs reign supreme, rampant in My "church" that is supposed to be a place of love and acceptance to equip My children to further the kingdom. What is more profitable, programs, or equipping them in the Holy Spirit? You do not build your "church," I build the Church.

Stop sacrificing My children upon the altar of mammon, the altar of bigger buildings, competing with one another to be the biggest and the best. There is no competition in My kingdom. I build. I give, I take away. I will restore a heart, completely mine. Turn from your wicked ways, for judgment starts in the house of God.

My children need help and healing, not more burdens heaped upon them, not more building programs. Go back to basics. Heal the sick of heart, mind, body and soul. Feed the hungry, and care for the orphans and widows, that is your calling. Spread the gospel message. Be the gospel message. Do not build ivory towers that keep you in and Me out. I want to come to "church."

Stop denying the presence, the leading, the Helper; Holy Spirit. Let Him move in your midst. Let Him be free to be who He is. Stop worrying what the people will think. They should be worried Holy Spirit is not welcome, not what their peers believe.

A new thing that is an old thing. When did I lose control of My church? The day man wanted to go his own way. Words from the pulpit tickle ears, and warm hearts and minds, but they are words of man and not words of power or fire of My presence upon them.

Empty words and empty lives, not moving in the power of the Spirit. I commanded the early church to wait for the power from on high, yet the Helper and power from on high is no longer seen as necessary in Christendom today. The world looks on and says, "so what is the difference? You live and act no different than we do." We read the Bible and see what happened in those days, but we don't see it in these days. Why? Because you pick and choose words, afraid to offend the very ones I called you to lead. Why are you not afraid of offending Me?

My children, pique your ears and hear the word of the Lord. I am the Lord your God, and it's time to do it My way. Stop where you are and seek My face. Stop the routine that never changes. The Sunday morning routine hasn't changed; it is fixture in the church. What do you want, routine and tradition of men, or a fresh wave of My Spirit that will truly change hearts and minds to live for Me, full of My Spirit, empowered to impact the kingdom in multiplied ways?

There is a time of grace. Do not make the mistake of carrying on church as usual, not seeking My face; preaching canned sermons, rather than Holy Spirit fire. I long to fill you fresh with the new wine, to anoint your head with new oil, to impact the world in the way you dreamed about in your early days of ministry. It is necessary to go back to your dream, to go forward. Unleash the Spirit within your church and watch the changes come, watch the anointing flow, watch what you have longed for come to pass...not the dreams of man, but the fulfillment of your God. Nebuchadnezzar was of the opinion that he built the kingdom. It was a difficult lesson, but he learned, and was restored for the glory of My kingdom. My child, working so hard in your own strength, use Mine and you will no longer feel a burden, for My burden is light.

March 18, 2011

REST

REST! Rest My children in My arms of love. I am not a distant God. I am your Father God, and in Me you have your being. God of your yesterdays and your tomorrows, I am the present of your present. A gift of love into this world, each of you contains that seed of My love planted within your hearts to be multiplied and reseeded into the lives of others, to let My love transfer from person to person until it fills the earth.

The lives of My people are a gift to this world, a world of hurting hearts and minds, and a world of dying people. Dreams are dying around the globe. Despair is rampant. You are the light of My love to a dying world, those dying dreams. You are encouragement to the lives of those you meet. You are life to the dying hopes and dreams, food to the hunger pangs that go unfulfilled in the lives of those who do not know Me.

You are life, you have the answer. The hunger is rising. Can you feel it? The desperation, crying out for answers. What is going on in the world today? Why is this happening? There is no safety and security, they cry. You don't have to guess or wonder, you know the truth, and the truth sets you free.

Share the truth. Use your voice to set the captives free from fear. Proclaim life into their dead circumstances. When your words proceed from your mouth, new life will begin to flourish as a resurrection seed in the midst of hopeless circumstances. New life will spring forth as you proclaim My word into the atmosphere. See the tide of hope come in? The waves are getting bigger and bigger for those in Me. Give them the answers. Show them how to ride the waves of hope to the safety of the shore, the safety of My arms, and the safety of My love. Show them the safety of My blood.

Mighty warriors, arise. The time for passivity has long passed. Are you in the army of the Lord? Put your armor on and march to the highways and byways, you soldiers of the word. Proclaim My word, proclaim My name, for I am the resurrection and the only hope for the lost, the scared, the insecure; those who don't see a way out of their circumstances. I am the only One who can raise them from the ashes of their circumstances. I am reaching My hand, My mighty right hand, to pick those up who have fallen, to revive and strengthen their hearts and minds, to give strength to their legs to stand in the face of opposition.

Warriors, unite! In one accord, stand and hold hands and hearts like a chain of faith across this nation. Speak as one voice. Praise as one voice. Worship as one mighty chorus across the land to break the strong holds, to set the captives free, to stand, pray, and praise in the gap for those who cannot find their voices, for those who cannot stand on their own as their strength is little. Watch as this chain of faith spreads around the world.

My remnant, who refuse to compromise My word, who refuse to compromise the faith in the face of man, who do not seek popularity, but a heart surrendered to the Lord their God. You are the front lines. Stop being on the defense and go on the offense. The angels surround you. The battles lines have been drawn, the victory is sure.

March 20, 2011

NEW LEVEL

I am the Lord your God, and today I say:

I am the Lord your God and I call you unto Myself, to a new level of intimacy, to a new level of hearing and seeing in My Spirit, to a new level in Me. I call you to rise up and conquer those things that have seemed to be winning in your life, those situations which have caused pain, those situations that I have allowed to grow you and prepare you for the next level in Me. Arise. Arise in Me.

March 29, 2011

FREE

I woke to the words "You are free. You are free. FREEDOM! There has been a major shift in the Spirit".

Free in Me. Freedom in Me. You have been chained to debt, chained to people, chained to the law, chained and in bondage without even knowing the depth of your bondage to the entrapment of the enemy. Free in Me, free in Me. I call you to be free in Me; to break the chains of the heart and mind that have you bound. Let My spirit lead you into freedom; freedom from disease, freedom from emotional and physical pain. I long to heal you and make you well. Free in Me, free in Me, free in Me, I speak to the storms in your life, "Peace, be still." Let My spirit rise up within you for a mighty work in your life, to impact the kingdom for My glory.

We are free in Christ, at least we are supposed to be. Declare it aloud, this day, "I am free! I am free! FREEDOM!"

March 31, 2011

FEAR THE LORD

I am the Lord your God, and today I say this:

My hand is upon you. I will never leave you nor forsake you. I am in your midst and the kingdom of God is shaking. If I am was not in your midst, there would not be this kind of shaking. The powers of darkness are trembling. You can see it everywhere you look, for they know time is short. If you feel the shaking, you know that I am is in your midst, so rest, assured in Me.

Stand on My words; move in My spirit and you will receive divine impartation of new levels of power and authority. Watch what you say for it will surely come to pass. The powers of darkness tremble. They know this will come to pass when My people finally come into their own, a realization of who they are in Me, and stand and fight in the name of the God of the angel armies.

The battle belongs to Me, but you have a part to play. Believe, stand in faith, obey the Spirit, and you will find the angel armies are in your midst in a way you did not think possible. You will feel their presence surround you. Boldness to speak My word will come forth, and My glory will be released in unprecedented ways.

You have My authority. Behold, I have given you power over all the power of the enemy. Speak like it, walk like it, talk like it. Hold your head high. I have not left you. I have been strengthening you. Desert times make you stronger, build your faith, separate those who believe and have faith, and those who don't.

Weaknesses are revealed and exposed. What will you do with them? Keep as you are, or turn to Me? I am the answer to every question. I am the answer to every problem. I am the answer to every doubt. I am the answer to every fear. Fear is not faith. The word of God shines light into all circumstances. You are not in darkness as the unbelievers are in darkness. You know the end from the beginning. My grace is sufficient for you to prosper in these times. I desire you prosper.

Step out of doubt and into faith. Be unshakable. The earth may be shaking around you, but I am in your midst. Like an unruly child throwing a temper tantrum, the enemy is looking for your attention. Focus on Me, not your circumstances, and ignore the distractions and the tantrums. The more you ignore, the louder it gets for a while.

Prophesy to your circumstances; peace be still, the battle belongs to the Lord. Fear not, for I have redeemed you; I have called you by your name. You are mine. When you pass through the waters, I will be with you; through the rivers, they shall not overflow you. When you walk through the fire, you shall not be burned, nor shall the flame scorch you.

Speak My word, for My word has power over the darkness. They cannot argue My word, just your faith in My Word. See with eyes of faith, with feet firmly placed in My Word. Speak words of faith in the authority of the name of Jesus, for all must bow to the name of Jesus; sickness, disease, oppression.

Prophesy the word of God over yourself and your circumstances. Set the enemy on notice; you stand on the Word of God. You will not be shaken, although all around you shakes. Though circumstances appear the opposite of how they should be, it's just a temper tantrum, the kicking and screaming of the enemy is to get you to take your eyes off Me, to get you to move out of faith. If you look real close, he is not crying. He is laughing at you, mocking you. He thinks you are foolhardy. He may laugh now, but I am strengthening My children to stop watching the tantrums, to ignore them. Soon the enemy will realize you will not play the game and move on.

Be quick to profess My word over all your circumstances. He cannot prevent you from fulfilling your destiny in Me unless you let him. Walk with Me, talk to Me, allow Me to strengthen you to run the race. Angel cake I gave to Elijah when he grew weary. You will finish the race. The king is cheering you on. Holy Spirit is guiding the way. The angels are your front and rear guard. Whom shall you fear? Fear the Lord!

April 1, 2011

Vision:

BALLS OF FIRE IN NEW YORK

Last night I had a very disturbing vision.

I was escorted into a darkened room where a man was standing next to a movie screen and projector. He had white hair, a white shirt, a black tie, black pants, and dark glasses. He looked very governmental. He was holding a long pointer in his hand. He looked at me, pointed, and tapped the screen.

A vividly-colored video appeared displaying New York. It was beautiful, but instead of watching the movie, I suddenly found myself "flying" over New York City. We flew past the Statue of Liberty, up the river, then around Manhattan. I was amazed at how charming and serene things were.

All of a sudden, I saw missiles flying into New York City from the East, followed by fire ball after fire ball of explosions. This was quite real to me, and although it could have a spiritual meaning, I have concern that this could be literal and come to pass. Although, dreams, visions, and prophetic words often have many layers of meaning, I believe this was a warning given for intercession. Pray for the people and the city, and against this attack.

April 4, 2011

I Pour Out My Spirit Afresh

Truly, I pour My spirit out afresh and anew. People are dying every day without Me; living without hope, when hope and dreams are available to live inside them. Though they are in the midst of turmoil, hope is available just for the asking. I withhold nothing good from My children. I long to give so much, but so few want to receive, refusing to seek truth; believing lies that rob them of the blessings and the life I intended for them.

Do you want all, or are you content with a piece? Are you content with living in a lie the enemy has perpetrated to cheat you out of My grace, My gifts, My blessings, My power and My authority? Walk in My fullness. I am the Lord your God and things are about to change in your life.

Fruition of hopes and dreams; an activation. As spring births new life, I birth new life in My people. Will you receive Me and what I long to pour out, or will you reject the gift of Myself, analyzing what is for today or what is not? What I will do or not do? Receive the outpouring of My Spirit like a child full of wonder and excitement on Christmas day, or as a birthday gift, for I birth new life within you. Spring in the natural and in the supernatural.

April 10, 2011

VALLEY OF KIDRON

PART 1

This morning, I was awakened at 4:42 a.m., with the words of the Lord: "The Valley of Kidron lies before you." I have been hearing that repeatedly since waking.

I researched Kidron Valley and found it is also called the Valley of Jehoshaphat, or The Valley of Decision. It means *Jehovah is judge.*

The "Valley of Jehoshaphat" is the valley the world will be focused on in the Final Conflict, called Armageddon. The name Jehoshaphat is found only a few times in Biblical history. The Valley of Jehoshaphat is mentioned specifically only twice in scripture, both times in relation to prophecy as the Lord's end-time judgment upon the enemies of Israel.

Jehoshaphat is a Hebrew word, pronounced *yeh-haw-shaw-fawt,* a combination of two Hebrew words, *yeh-ho-vaw*, meaning **Jehovah,** *and Shaw-fat*, meaning **to judge**. Therefore, the word Jehoshaphat literally means, "**The Lord judges**."

Joel 3:1-2 *For, behold, in those days, and in that time, when I shall bring again the captivity of Judah and Jerusalem, I will also gather all nations, and will bring them down into **the valley of Jehoshaphat,** and will plead with them there for My people and for My heritage Israel, whom they have scattered among the nations, and parted My land.*

Joel 3:9-12 *Proclaim ye this among the Gentiles; Prepare war, wake up the mighty men, let all the men of war draw near; let them come up: Beat your plowshares into swords, and your pruning hooks into spears: let the weak say, I am strong. Assemble* *yourselves, and come, all ye heathen, and gather yourselves together round about: thither cause thy mighty ones to come down, O LORD. Let the heathen be wakened, and* **come up to the valley of Jehoshaphat***: for* **there will I sit to judge** *all the heathen round about. Put ye in the sickle, for the harvest is ripe: come, get you down; for the press is full, the vats overflow; for their wickedness is great.* **Multitudes, multitudes in the valley of decision***: for the day of The Lord is near in the valley of decision."*

Jeremiah 31:40 (NKJV) *⁴⁰And the whole valley of the dead bodies and of the ashes, and all the fields as far as the Brook Kidron, to the corner of the Horse Gate toward the east, shall be holy to the LORD. It shall not be plucked up or thrown down anymore forever."*

Most of the other scriptures on the Kidron Valley talk about tearing down the pagan altars and symbols.

It is pretty clear the valley of decision, where God will sit and judge man, lies before us. Will we tear down the pagan idols in our lives and our nation? Will we step into kingdom mentality and focus? Will we stand in faith, speaking life into the dead bones?

As I have previously explained, God's definition of prosperity is not about money. It can include money, but God is more interested in our hearts and our lives prospering in Him.
This word followed the above revelation:

I am the Lord your God, and today I say; I am the God of your todays and tomorrow's, the Alpha and Omega, for I know your end from your beginning. Let that revelation be your peace. Stop striving; rest in Me. You are My child, flesh of My flesh and bone of My bone. I made you in the very likeness of Me. Flesh of My flesh and bone of My bone, I formed you with My two hands in your mother's womb. I put you together, for I know the plans I have for you; a future and a hope.

The Kidron Valley stands before you. Cross through the Valley, into the valley of hopes and dreams. You have been afraid to dream, afraid to believe, but I have been restoring hopes and dreams over recent days, for without vision My people perish.

The enemy has worked hard to remove your hopes and dreams, and make them seem like the impossible. I am the giver of life, the giver of hopes and dreams, and I am restoring that which you thought was dead. Hope springs eternal, for I am the God of hope who lives within you. Hope springs eternal for I am the God of hope.

Hopefulness is invading the desert place. Prophesy to the dry bones of your soul to live again. Loose fertile blood stained soil of My Spirit. Resurrect those dreams you thought were dead. The economy is of no effect, for in My economy there is no lack. The enemy of your soul tried to convince you that you must settle for less than My very best, that you must settle and should be grateful for just barely getting by. I am the Lord your God, the God of more than enough, an abundance of all things.

I want you to prosper in your marriages, in your finances, in your ministries, and not settle. The problem is many do not believe prosperity is possible, overwhelmed in your circumstances or the circumstances that surround you. The Valley of Indecision has trampled hopes and dreams as it does not look like the right time to prosper. It looks like the time to settle for less; whatever you can get, just to squeak by, but I never intended for My children to live like that. Purge all that is not of Me from your life, for it is the Kingdom key to move out of your current circumstances and into the future. The enemy has been playing "pickle" with you, trying to wear you out and wear you down, keeping the dream just out of reach. You have no idea how close you are to breakthrough.

The Kidron Valley stands before you. It is a place of dead bones, a place of Messiah returns. It is a place of hope, to watch and wait for My return. Be about My business while you wait. Prosper in all things. Your bridegroom waits at the door. I am coming soon.

What you do not fully understand is that circumstances can change in the blink of an eye. I am returning in the blink of an eye. Reprioritize your life and thinking, move into the kingdom mentality. Reach the hurting and the lost. I resurrect hopes and dreams to carry you through these times, hope for My soon return. The seeds of hope; to reach the lost and hurting through the power of My gospel message, the power of My Word, the power of My authority upon the earth. Move in it.

Speak to the darkness that surrounds you. Speak to the darkness that invades the hearts and minds of those around you. You are a force to be reckoned with in the earth, to invade lives with the light of My presence. It shines through you. The Kidron Valley lies before you, My child. Do not lose heart. Be watchful, waiting. Be about My business, for I release signs and wonders to follow My children. It will be as in the days of old; watch what you say, for your words have power. When you speak, it will be as if I speak.

April 24, 2011

FAITH ARISE

The minute I opened My eyes this morning, I heard these words:

"I AM resurrecting the seeds of finance."

Later during worship today, I heard, "Let your faith arise. As I rose from the dead, resurrect all those things in your heart. All those seeds that have fallen to the ground, those seeds planted, let faith arise to resurrect them in your life. Resurrect your hopes and dreams as the seeds sprout in your heart and your mind. Let faith arise as new life springs forth, this day, as that which was once dormant springs to life".

May 1, 2011

TURN AROUND

You have been loyal and faithful, obedient to My word and what I have called you to do. Things will turn around for you. Unexpected turnaround in ways you would never expect. Look for the turnaround to begin in the little things in life, and these little things will become big things as My Spirit moves in your life. Cast your cares and worry not, for I have your life in the palm of My hand. Ask and you shall receive.

May 6, 2011

RESTORING HOPE

I am restoring hope to My children. Faith is the substance of things hoped for. Without hope, there can be no faith. Without faith, mountains don't move, and the lame do not walk. Hope is a mainstay. Hope springs eternal. It is a small word with mighty implications of My kingdom.

Allow yourself to hope. Many of you have buried hope. Along with that, you bury faith and impede your future. Dare to breathe, My children, dare to breathe. Some of you have been holding your spiritual breath; you are in stall mode, unable to dream or believe to move forward, overwhelmed with all you see.

Breathe again. Start putting one foot in front of the other and move. Move as Abraham moved. He moved in faith. He did not know where he was going, but he moved because I said move. That should be enough for you, My child, The fact I said move. Put your hand into Mine. Restart the journey. I am with you!

BURNING LOVE

I love you with an everlasting love, a burning love unsurpassed. Feel the depth of My love for you, it's a love so deep you cannot fully understand. It's a love so deep My heart burns in My chest towards you. I want you to love Me with that burning kind of love, from the depth of your very being. Hunger for Me. Hunger for more of Me, reach out and receive My love for you. My heart burns for you, My child. My heart delights in you. I anxiously wait to hear a word from you, to know I am on your heart.

Sing to me, My child, I long to hear a song of love. Praise Me, My child, for all My love pours out upon you. I will withhold no good thing from you; *no* good thing. My heart burns for you, My child. I burn with love for you!

Set your flame to burn with the fire of My love in the lives of all those who surround you. Show your love to the world, for it is My love that will reach them, not words. Your love will speak louder than words. A demonstration of love requires no words. Look no further than the message of the cross. It requires no words; hearts understand the depth of love it takes to die a brutal death. To give one's life on behalf of another is love in its truest form. Give a loaf of bread to the hungry, a smile and a touch of the hand to those hurting, a listening ear, a giving heart. Serve Me. It is all done in service to Me; do it unto Me. Let My love burn through you to reach the hurting and the lost.

May 19, 2011

THE MEASURING LINE IS IN HIS HAND

PART 1

A few months ago, I picked up the Bible to read and the Lord spoke **Zechariah 2:1**, which says, *"Then I looked up, and there before me was a man with a measuring line in his hand."* If one goes on to read the rest of the chapter, God was going to measure Jerusalem, yet the Lord only gave me verse 1 at that time. God intended to measure something. I was not certain if it was the church, the nation, or the world.

Seeking clarity through prayer, I learned that God was taking out a measuring stick as a way to see if we measure up. There is no condemnation for those in Christ, yet one does not have to think very hard to realize we have sorely failed as a nation, with an anti-God agenda seeking to remove God from every aspect of public life. Inch by inch, God's blessing is being removed as a result.

The people have donated their gold and riches to construct a golden calf on the altars of the churches. Their hearts are deceived, serving a God who can neither, speak or hear. We have failed as a church, with pastors, evangelists, and prophets who behave like movie stars, looking for people to serve them, vying for attention, more money, and larger buildings. They are not pointing the way to Christ. They are not glorifying the Lord. They are behaving like our government of late, Czars lording over the people, demanding people serve them rather than serving the people. The way some in the church are behaving, it reminds me of the scriptures where Paul spoke;

1 Corinthians: 10-13, *I appeal to you, brothers and sisters, in the name of our Lord Jesus Christ, that all of you agree with one another in what you say and that there be no divisions among you, but that you be perfectly united in mind and thought. My brothers and sisters, some from Chloe's household have informed me that there are quarrels among you. What I mean is this: One of you says, "I follow Paul"; another, "I follow Apollos"; another, "I follow Cephas"; still another, "I follow Christ." Is Christ divided? Was Paul crucified for you? Were you baptized in the name of Paul?*

Paul was basically saying; Gee, I am glad I did not baptize you, as you are quarreling among yourselves over a man and his teaching. You are following a man, substituting a man for God.

God is taking out the measuring stick and we have fallen short. We have been found wanting.

Two nights ago, I again picked up the bible to read and the Lord spoke to me; **Zechariah 4:1-6**. It reads; *1 Then the angel who talked with me returned and woke me up, like someone awakened from sleep. 2 He asked me, "What do you see?" I answered, "I see a solid gold lamp stand with a bowl at the top and seven lamps on it, with seven channels to the lamps. 3 Also there are two olive trees by it, one on the right of the bowl and the other on its left." 4 I asked the angel who talked with me, "What are these, my lord?" 5 He answered, "Do you not know what these are?" "No, my lord," I replied. 6 So he said to me, "This is the word of the LORD to Zerubbabel: 'Not by might nor by power, but by my Spirit,' says the LORD Almighty.*

Zechariah was seeing the Menorah in the Temple. The seven oil channels represent the seven fold aspect of Holy Spirit, as described by Jesus in **Isaiah 11: 1-3**;

The Spirit of the LORD will rest on him— the Spirit of wisdom and of understanding, the Spirit of counsel and of might, the Spirit of the knowledge and fear of the LORD and he will delight in the fear of the LORD.

And as I read those scriptures, the Lord began to show me clearly that we as a nation, we as a church, and we as individuals are working very hard to do things in our own strength, rather than relying on Holy Spirit. We have walked away from the Lord, choosing to do things our way, rather than His way. As we just read, it clearly stated in Zechariah, *'Not by might nor by power, but by my Spirit,' says the LORD Almighty.*

Just as the enemy always has a counterfeit, he has perverted the hearts and minds of men by people seeking out pastors, evangelists and prophets. They removed the focus from Christ as the head of the church. These people are placed by God to point the way to Christ, not take away. People are seeking out a word from man, rather than hearing from God themselves. I hear people saying; "go here, go there, see they are in revival," running from conference to conference for something they already have access to; the Lord God and Holy Spirit. If the Lord is not "moving" in a powerful way in our churches or ministries, there is no one to blame but us. God does not hold anything back from us.

That which hinders a powerful move of God is us; you and I. Our doubts, our fears, our failing to spend time worshipping God and reading His word. God wants to move as much in small town America as he does in large cities.

When we are in Christ, the sevenfold Holy Spirit lives in us, as it did in Jesus. Holy Spirit has been marginalized in many of the churches. When I say churches, I know that *we* are the church, *we* are body of Christ, but I am talking about what goes on in the four walls of the buildings we like to call the "church" in America. Yet, we wonder why there is no move of God? Man has replaced Christ as the head of the church in America. The enemy has made significant inroads. In our churches we see the cross removed, Holy Spirit unnecessary, the blood rarely mentioned, and the resurrection referred to in a once per year sermon.

I heard Jack Van Impe was releasing the names of 20 or so popular, well known Pastors, who have removed the message of the cross in "their" churches. They advocate removal of the cross to make church more attractive to the masses; to be "seeker friendly." The power that comes through each of us, through Holy Spirit, has been perverted and replaced by reliance on self.

I was watching an interview with a gentleman who is with the Church of Satan. He was asked what the Church of Satan was about. To my surprise, he never mentioned the worship of Satan. He said it was about the worship of self; doing what you want to do, when you want to do it, how you want to do it. It is worship of self, self-gratification, he explained. How is that different from our local "churches" today?

We can see that selfish mentality increasing throughout the decades, and we can see it very clearly in the church in America. Few churches support missions, few are focused on outreach or evangelism, and few take care of the widows, orphans, and those in need. God never intended for it to be that way. Our churches and believers are not to be internally focused, but Christ focused. Focus on Christ will cause our hearts to focus outward, serving others and reaching them for the kingdom. God never intended the "churches" to be focused within the four walls, waiting for the world to come to them.

The nation came seeking the church after 9/11. It found a church much like the world, wholly unprepared for the influx of people asking questions and looking for answers. They were looking for the God of the Bible; the powerful, miracle-working God and His word. Instead, they found a "church," internally devoid of the power of the blood and the word. We were self-focused. If there is no change, as the darkness of the world deepens, the church will not be able to reach those lost and hurting who come for answers and healing.

Since that was never God's intent, I do not believe the churches that are internally focused will prosper in the seasons ahead. The only way a church will properly thrive in the future will be if it remains Christ-centered; outreach, missions, evangelically focused. It is a sad state of affairs, and I am sure the heart of God is grieved. I know my heart is grieved. I know there is a remnant of God's people out there who have not bowed their knee to Baal, whose eyes are focused on Christ at the right hand of the Father, praying and interceding for His will be to be done on earth as it is in heaven, praying and interceding for His will to be done in the lives of the people, this nation, and His churches.

I have been hearing repeatedly from the Lord, *"Tell them to come out of her. Come out of her, My people"* (Revelation 18:4). Well, come out of what? Come out of this religious system where Christ is no longer the head of the church. If your church has lost its focus on Christ and is internally focused, or if you cannot remember the last time your Pastor preached about the blood, the cross, the resurrected Christ, or Holy Spirit, come out of her. It is time to stand up and be counted for God. It is time to stand up for the God you claim to serve. It is time to stand up and not be ashamed of the word of God. It is time to be speaking the word of God, reaching others for Christ, and challenging others around us to be servants of the most-high God.

It is time to allow and to advocate for God's agenda; to return His heart to the churches, to our hearts and minds, and to this nation. All around the world, in our families, schools and government, how can this be accomplished? It all starts in the heart of each one of us. It is only His love that can ignite a fire that will spread like a wildfire on the winds of the Spirit that can bring forth the changes. It is God who draws the heart of man to Himself.

Going back to **Zechariah 2**;

A Man With a Measuring Line *1 Then I looked up, and there before me was a man with a measuring line in his hand. 2 I asked, "Where are you going?"*

He answered me, "To measure Jerusalem, to find out how wide and how long it is."

3 While the angel who was speaking to me was leaving, another angel came to meet him 4 and said to him: "Run, tell that young man, 'Jerusalem will be a city without walls because of the great number of people and animals in it. 5 And I myself will be a wall of fire around it,' declares the LORD, 'and I will be its glory within.'

6 "Come! Come! Flee from the land of the north," declares the LORD, "for I have scattered you to the four winds of heaven," declares the LORD.

7 "Come, Zion! Escape, you who live in Daughter Babylon!" 8 For this is what the LORD Almighty says: "After the Glorious One has sent me against the nations that have plundered you—for whoever touches you touches the apple of his eye— 9 I will surely raise my hand against them so that their slaves will plunder them. Then you will know that the LORD Almighty has sent me.

10 "Shout and be glad, Daughter Zion. For I am coming, and I will live among you," declares the LORD. 11 "Many nations will be joined with the LORD in that day and will become my people. I will live among you and you will know that the LORD Almighty has sent me to you. 12 The LORD will inherit Judah as his portion in the holy land and will again choose Jerusalem. 13 Be still before the LORD, all mankind, because he has roused himself from his holy dwelling."

We know this refers to the future of Jerusalem, but there is a message for us right now; come out of Babylon, the corrupt "church". God is going to scatter to the four winds those churches and people who are not about His business. God wants to break down the walls of the traditional church. He will be the wall of fire that surrounds His people; *His* church. He is our protection. His remnant is the apple of His eye and all those who raise a hand against His children, the true body of Christ, He will raise His hand against them. He is calling us to holiness, to return to Him and worship Him the way He intended. He is calling us to refuse to compromise; to follow God's ways and accept no substitute for the one true God.

May 20, 2011

THE MEASURING LINE IS IN HIS HAND

PART 2

BEFORE the Lord gave me the message yesterday about the Measuring Line is in His Hand, BEFORE I heard the terrible thing our President said about Israel, the Lord had given me a word.

I had no idea at the time I was scribing this word that our President, Barack Obama, had called for the division of Israel back to the 1967 borders. I stand with Israel and I am proud to do so; not because I am Jewish and my family is from the tribes of Judah and Napthali, but because Israel/Jerusalem is God's heart...it is *right* to be supporting her. I am deeply grieved over the recent events; our President refusing to meet with Netanyahu, even lying about not having the time to meet with him.

I am ashamed and embarrassed for our President and his arrogance. He is not speaking for the people of this nation. I have been grieved and crying out to the Lord for Israel and for mercy on this nation. Much of its "new" agenda is a far cry from the values most of us hold dear. I have asked God to forgive our leaders, and to forgive the people who were blinded to vote for the "change" that has been leading us on the road to destruction.

The Lord showed me Belshazzar on his throne, drunk, and the people partying as he called for the sacred challis and items from the temple. Disrespectful, treating the holy as common, all while the enemy was standing at the gates, ready to attack. This administration, in its mindboggling arrogance, has disrespected the precious apple of God's eye. They have also disrespected the leaders He has placed in power, treating them as common and disposable. Can you see God's handwriting on the wall?

Daniel 25: [23] *For you have proudly defied the Lord of heaven and have had these cups from his Temple brought before you. You and your nobles and your wives and concubines have been drinking wine from them while praising gods of silver, gold, bronze, iron, wood, and stone—gods that neither see nor hear nor know anything at all. But you have not honored the God who gives you the breath of life and controls your destiny!* [24] *So God has sent this hand to write this message.* [25] *"This is the message that was written: MENE, MENE, TEKEL, and PARSIN.* [26] *This is what these words mean: Mene means 'numbered'—God has numbered the days of your reign and has brought it to an end.* [27] *Tekel means 'weighed'—you have been weighed on the balances and have not measured up.* [28] *Parsin means 'divided'—your kingdom has been divided and given to the Medes and Persians."*

One thing I have learned clearly over the years, is that when the Lord gives a word there can be many layers and meanings that unfold over days, weeks, months, years and even decades. The Lord gave a word for the nation and the church yesterday. Today, He has given an addendum.

The word yesterday discussed the division in the nation and the division in the church. Now it speaks of the division of Israel. All three had been blessed and have held the position of "apple of God's eye." This nation and the church have turned against God, going their own way, as the nation of Israel did so many times in the past. God still loves us and His church, as He loves Israel. Just as in days past, God ALWAYS has a remnant, and the remnant has been crying out to Him as Abraham did, "Would you destroy the city for 10 righteous? There are more than 10 who love you Lord!"

As the scriptures yesterday from **Zechariah 2:1-2** states, *"Then I looked up, and there before me was a man with a measuring line in his hand." ² I asked, "Where are you going?" He answered me, "To measure Jerusalem, to find out how wide and how long it is."*

God has measured Jerusalem. He knows exactly how long and how wide Israel is, and it is NOT what man says the borders are. It is what God says the borders are in the original covenant!

Zechariah 2 continues, *³ While the angel who was speaking to me was leaving, another angel came to meet him ⁴ and said to him: "Run, tell that young man, 'Jerusalem will be a city without walls because of the great number of people and animals in it. ⁵ And I myself will be a wall of fire around it,' declares the LORD, 'and I will be its glory within.' ⁶ "Come! Come! Flee from the land of the north," declares the LORD, "for I have scattered you to the four winds of heaven," declares the LORD. ⁷ "Come, Zion! Escape, you who live in Daughter Babylon!" ⁸ For this is what the LORD Almighty says: "After the Glorious One has sent me against the nations that have plundered you—for whoever touches you touches the apple of his eye— ⁹ I will surely raise my hand against them so that their slaves will plunder them. Then you will know that the LORD Almighty has sent me.*

¹⁰ "Shout and be glad, Daughter Zion. For I am coming, and I will live among you," declares the LORD. ¹¹ "Many nations will be joined with the LORD in that day and will become my people. I will live among you and you will know that the LORD Almighty has sent me to you. ¹² The LORD will inherit Judah as his portion in the holy land and will again choose Jerusalem. ¹³ Be still before the LORD, all mankind, because he has roused himself from his holy dwelling."

God is the God of Israel, even if most of the population is secular and have not believed that. God scattered the people, but he has been calling them home from the four winds, calling them to *Aliyah* ("going up," or "ascent"), a call to immigration back to their Jewish homeland. He is the God of fire. He is the wall that surrounds the land and as in Zechariah 2: 8-9 (see above). God established Israel. If God establishes a thing, who is man to dare come against it?

God will raise His hand against this nation as He raised His hand against nations past who "poked him in the eye." He is a jealous Father. Just as with our own children, when they choose to do wrong, it upsets us, but we still love them. We still want to protect them and bless them. God does the same.

We cannot be deceived, God is no respecter of persons or nations. We have been taunting and taunting. Like bullies, we continue shaking our fists and pointing our fingers in His face in all our arrogance. There comes a point where the one who has quietly and patiently taken the abuse will stand up and confront the bully. If this nation and the church do not change our ways, the disasters, economic collapse, and attacks of the enemy will continue. God *will* get our attention. He will bring us to our knees, to get us to look up.

I fear it is fast becoming too late. God help us. God forgive us. Your remnant is crying out to you, Lord. The heart of your remnant aches, along with yours. God have mercy! I have said many times in the past, the next election will mark a dramatic turning point in this nation. In spite of the hardships we have faced in this nation, we are still in a time of grace. God granted the choices of the people to see if this is the direction we really wanted for this nation, or if we will see the error of our ways and turn back before it is too late. If you have eyes to see and ears to hear what the Spirit is saying, rise up and pray! Rise up and speak. Rise up and stand firm for what is right. Rise up and be the salt and the light to the church, to this nation, and to the world!

May 21, 2011

The Measuring Line Is In His Hand

Part 3:

One more revelation on this subject.

The Lord took me back to the word given April 10, 2011. At that time, the Lord had said, "The Valley of Kidron lies before you." This has to do with this period of continued grace, as mentioned in the previous word, part 2.

The Valley of Kidron refers to the Valley of Decision/Valley of Judgment which lies before us as individuals, a church, and a nation. I think it is pretty clear that in the Valley of Decision we ALL have to make the same choice; Whom will we serve? Too many are living and acting like the world, giving nothing more than lip service to the Lord. Something is seriously wrong when poll results indicate 83% of people claim to be Christians. When we look at the condition of the church and the world, we know that cannot be true. We will make a decision, or God will make it for us. The Valley of Decision and the Valley of Judgment are the same place, but I see it as two sides. We must make a decision. It is here that God will sit and judge us, and His judgment lies before us; it is at the door.

What will we decide? Will we tear down the pagan idols in our lives, our churches, and this nation? Will we step into a kingdom mentality and focus? Will we stand in faith? Will we speak life into the dead bones?

There is a decision to be made. Return to the Lord God who longs to bless His people, His Church, and this nation, or continue on the road to death and destruction.

May 22, 2011

Valley of Kidron

Part 2

The previous word on this subject talked about blessings, which I think God is saying He desires to pour out. God is warning us of what is to come. We can accept the offer for blessing or reject it, depending on our willingness or unwillingness to repent.

In a vision, the Lord showed me a freeway with people walking on smooth concrete. Then the road changed; it looked as if someone had dug up the concrete and left huge chunks in the road. The people began to work hard climbing over the chunks of concrete to continue walking, and the journey became slow and arduous. We are on a journey, which started out rather smooth. As a nation, we are walking, yet we are on a road meant for fast travel in vehicles. So, our journey has been slow, and required effort, but has still been smooth. The road then changed to a very difficult road to travel; as noted above, this is a warning.

The Lord spoke;

The Valley of Kidron lies before you as an individual, as a church, and as a nation. But, more than that, it is for the world. Nation, rise. March to the beat of My drum. Open your eyes and ears to hear what the Spirit is saying, for the end draws nigh. I am not playing. Stop playing "church," stop delaying, stop making excuses. The Valley of Kidron lies before you, nation. It lies before you, church. Which will you choose? Blessing or cursing?

The Valley of Kidron lies before, paved with obstacles from my adversary which are meant to block your way to blessing. There will be many decisions along the way as you maneuver your way through in the coming days, weeks, and months. The right decision always starts with Me. Come out from among her, My people, and move in Spirit. He will guide you safely home, for He was sent for such a time as this; to guide and maneuver you through the obstacles that block you from Me.

May 27, 2011

Vision:

PSALM 91 – TORNADO

Last night I had a vision. I was with people at a park. I stood up, looked over the western horizon, and saw a massive tornado. I watched it for a bit to see which direction it was heading. It was coming straight at us, so I yelled out a warning and people began to run.

I ran into a house with my family and we grabbed blankets and pillows, and hid in a small closet. We waited, but the tornado never came. We finally got up and looked out the closet and could see blue sky, though the house was still intact.

I have had many visions of tornados, with the words "winds of change" in the past, but this vision was a warning. Many terrible things are on the horizon that look like they are coming directly at God's people, but we just need to hide in the prayer closet, under the shadow of His wings, and the storm will pass us by.

He is our rock and our fortress. He tells us in Psalm 91 that if we, you and I, do as instructed in the first two verses; dwell in His secret place and abide, then He will do as He said in the rest of the verses. How awesome is that?! IT CAN'T GET ANY BETTER THAN THAT! I love our Lord!!

Psalm 91 - Safety of Abiding in the Presence of God

IF we do the first two verses;

1 He who dwells in the secret place of the Most High Shall abide under the shadow of the Almighty.
2 I will say of the LORD, "He is My refuge and My fortress; My God, in Him I will trust."

156

THEN, God will do the rest;

3 Surely He shall deliver you from the snare of the fowler
And from the perilous pestilence.
4 He shall cover you with His feathers, And under His wings you
shall take refuge; His truth shall be your shield and buckler.
5 You shall not be afraid of the terror by night, Nor of the arrow
that flies by day,
6 Nor of the pestilence that walks in darkness, Nor of the
destruction that lays waste at noonday.
7 A thousand may fall at your side, And ten thousand at your right
hand; But it shall not come near you. 8 Only with your eyes shall
you look, And see the reward of the wicked.
9 Because you have made the LORD, who is My refuge, Even the
Most High, your dwelling place,
10 No evil shall befall you, Nor shall any plague come near your
dwelling;
11 For He shall give His angels charge over you, To keep you in all
your ways.
12 In their hands they shall bear you up, Lest you dash your foot
against a stone.
13 You shall tread upon the lion and the cobra, The young lion and
the serpent you shall trample underfoot.
14 "Because he has set his love upon Me,
therefore I will deliver him; I will set him on high, because he has
known My name.
15 He shall call upon Me, and I will answer him; I will be with him
in trouble; I will deliver him and honor him.
16 With long life I will satisfy him,
And show him My salvation."

May 28, 2011

JEREMIAH 5

I have been hearing the Lord repeatedly and clearly saying; **"Jeremiah 5."**

As we discussed in the previous word series called "The Measuring Line," Abraham sought mercy when he was told of the imminent destruction of Sodom and Gomorrah. He asked if God would destroy them if there were 10 righteous in the city. God did not find 10 righteous and the cities were destroyed. Jeremiah found himself in a similar situation. He wrote these words of the Lord;

1 "Go up and down the streets of Jerusalem, look around and consider, search through her squares. If you can find but one person who deals honestly and seeks the truth, I will forgive this city. 2 Although they say, 'As surely as the LORD lives,' still they are swearing falsely." 3 LORD, do not your eyes look for truth? You struck them, but they felt no pain; you crushed them, but they refused correction. They made their faces harder than stone and refused to repent. 4 I thought, "These are only the poor; they are foolish, for they do not know the way of the LORD, the requirements of their God. 5 So I will go to the leaders and speak to them; surely they know the way of the LORD, the requirements of their God." But with one accord they too had broken off the yoke and torn off the bonds.

This nation has suffered unprecedented shaking in blow after blow since 2001. We had 9/11; hurricanes named Andrew, Katrina, and Rita; flooding, snow storms, droughts, and other unusual weather patterns; economic devastation, and on and on. We live under rogue governmental and church leadership. This nation has been struck, yet the people continue to swear falsely.

They are not looking to the Lord for truth. We have been struck severely, but seemingly felt no pain, or the pain has been quickly forgotten. We have not learned.

The faces of this government and its people have been hardened, refusing to repent. The government and the church have become foolish, wise only in the arrogance of their own eyes. The Lord has been speaking to our leaders, and He is reminding us about **Jeremiah 5:5**, *I will go and speak to their leaders. Surely they will know the LORD's ways and what God requires of them." But the leaders, too, had utterly rejected their God (NLT).*

Why? For the reasons Paul discussed in **1 Corinthians:18-19** *For the message of the cross is foolishness to those who are perishing, but to us who are being saved it is the power of God. For it is written: "I will destroy the wisdom of the wise; the intelligence of the intelligent I will frustrate."*

The government of this nation has been hijacked by anti-God agendas and human wisdom. The basic belief in God which was the foundation of this nation, established in *The Mayflower Compact* even before settlement, has been decaying for decades. In just two short years, the crumbling of the foundation has progressed rapidly. The wall of protection around this nation is battered and broken, breached by the enemy. The message of the cross is no longer integral to the church that bears HIS name.

The true believer is now considered an enemy of the government. Evangelical Christians have now found themselves on the Homeland Security terrorist list, and we ask the same questions Paul did in **1 Corinthians: 1:20**, *"Where is the wise person? Where is the teacher of the law? Where is the philosopher of this age? Has not God made foolish the wisdom of the world?"* All the while knowing the answer is as valid today, as it was then, Paul continues, *"For since in the wisdom of God, the world through its wisdom did not know him, God was pleased through the* *foolishness of what was preached to save those who believe.* ²² *Jews demand signs and Greeks look for wisdom,* ²³ *but we preach Christ crucified: a stumbling block to Jews and foolishness to Gentiles,* ²⁴ *but to those whom God has called, both Jews and Greeks, Christ the power of God and the wisdom of God.* ²⁵ *For the foolishness of God is wiser than human wisdom, and the weakness of God is stronger than human strength."*

The world in all its presumed knowledge, in all its arrogance and self-proclaimed wisdom, is nothing but foolishness in the eyes of God, particularly when viewed with eternity in mind.

Jeremiah 5:6-9 expresses, *Therefore, a lion from the forest will attack them, a wolf from the desert will ravage them, a leopard will lie in wait near their towns to tear to pieces any who venture out, for their rebellion is great and their backslidings many. "Why should I forgive you? Your children have forsaken me and sworn by gods that are not gods. I supplied all their needs, yet they committed adultery and thronged to the houses of prostitutes. They are well-fed, lusty stallions, each neighing for another man's wife. Should I not punish them for this?" declares the LORD. "Should I not avenge Myself on such a nation as this?*

My heart is breaking as I read from Jeremiah and write these words. Yes, the children of this nation have forsaken the Lord. I read some stats from 10 years ago, that only 4% of the youth serve the Lord, while 32% of their parents do. God has dealt generously with this nation. Its churches have been blessed beyond measure. We have lived with abundance in every area of our lives. This nation and the church, for a time, was the envy and the light of nations; sending out missionaries into the four corners of the world. Now, the Lord is sending missionaries *to* the United States! So God continued;

10 *"Go through her vineyards and ravage them, but do not destroy them completely. Strip off her branches, for these people do not belong to the LORD.*

The abundance this nation enjoyed is being stripped away. The abundance of blessing meant to further God's kingdom and His agenda has been wasted on useless things; bigger and better toys, cars, and boats...the gluttonous pursuit of mammon, and self-worship, while some live in squalor; on the street, hungry, without even basic necessities. Our church buildings have grown to massive proportions and the focus has turned inward, toward accumulating wealth and building kingdoms on the altar of self, rather than being the hands and heart of God, serving those in need.

Our priorities are out of line with those of God, Who provided the abundance of blessing in the first place. The God we claim to serve never intended for us to accumulate wealth, filling the storehouses just to build bigger ones. The blessing was intended to be passed through our hands as individuals, the church, and this nation, shared in God's bounty. We failed the test of servant-hood. *To whom much is given, much is required* (**Luke 12:48**). We will give an account of what we have done with the "talents" we were given. Many have been buried or wasted rather than invested in the economy of the kingdom and the lives of those in need (**Matthew 25**).

We can clearly see the shortages of food, water, and oil on the horizon. The vineyards are slowly being ravaged. Praise the Lord we will not be destroyed completely, but many people have been brought to their knees in recent years as the economy and all that can be shaken is being shaken.

Before this economic crash, the Lord gave me a word about the shaking. He told me that people were out there rebuking the enemy, but it was HIM doing the shaking, not the enemy. They did not want to hear it. They asked, disbelieving, *Why would the Lord shake this nation*? They were angry at the messenger. These scriptures in **Jeremiah 5:11-18** answer that question clearly;

11 The people of Israel and the people of Judah have been utterly unfaithful to me," declares the LORD. 12 They have lied about the LORD; they said, "He will do nothing! No harm will come to us; we will never see sword or famine. 13 The prophets are but wind and the word is not in them; so let what they say be done to them." 14 Therefore this is what the LORD God Almighty says: "Because the people have spoken these words, I will make My words in your mouth a fire and these people the wood it consumes. 15 People of Israel," declares the LORD, "I am bringing a distant nation against you — an ancient and enduring nation, a people whose language you do not know, whose speech you do not understand.

16 Their quivers are like an open grave; all of them are mighty warriors. 17 They will devour your harvests and food, devour your sons and daughters; they will devour your flocks and herds, devour your vines and fig trees. With the sword they will destroy the fortified cities in which you trust. 18 "Yet even in those days," declares the LORD, "I will not destroy you completely.

We have seen the rise of radical Islam over the past decade. We did not think too much about what was going on in the Mideast except for how it affected Israel. We did not think it would be something we would see; an enemy infiltrating this nation and our highest levels of government. We did not think we would see attacks on our own soil. More than that, the unthinkable ~ calls for Sharia Law in the United States of America! The rise of secular humanism is growing rapidly.

On September 9, 2012, we watched as our embassies burned and our ambassadors were murdered; it was blamed on a movie. Rather than standing upon our Bill of Rights, Constitution and

God-given freedoms as human beings, we apologized as a nation to try and appease the enemy of our souls. Since then, we have learned that the lies and deceit were pervasive and extensive, intended to defraud not just the American people, but the world.

In this 5th chapter of Jeremiah, we read that God said He would do five things:

1) I will visit the nation.

2) I will avenge this nation.

3) I will send destruction.

4) Twice he said he will not make a full end.

5) Her battlements will be taken away, because the nation had dealt very treacherously and they acted deceitfully against the Lord.

The people said it was not God who had spoken by the prophets.

I was asked many times *why* the Lord would shake this nation. As I said earlier, the Lord had made it clear, HE was the one who was shaking this nation...to get our eyes back on Him, to get our priorities back in line with His, to be the people He intended His children to be. Those who profess to be His have been living like the world. Those in the world and even in the church do not fear Him, and His Word tells us it is a fearful thing to fall into the hands of the living God.

19 And when the people ask, 'Why has the LORD our God done all this to us?' You will tell them, 'As you have forsaken me and served foreign gods in your own land so you shall serve aliens in a land that is not yours.' 20 "Announce this to the descendants of Jacob and proclaim it in Judah: 21 Hear this, you foolish and senseless people, who have eyes but do not see, who have ears but do not hear: 22 Should you not fear me?" declares the LORD. "Should you not tremble in My presence? I made the sand a boundary for the sea, an everlasting barrier it cannot cross. The waves may roll, but they cannot prevail; they may roar, but they cannot cross it. ²³ But these people have stubborn and rebellious hearts; they have turned aside and gone away. ²⁴ They do not say to themselves, 'Let us fear the LORD our God, who gives autumn and spring rains in season, who assures us of the regular weeks of harvest.' ²⁵ Your wrongdoings have kept these away; your sins have deprived you of good.

Secular humanism, Baal, self, and mammon are the gods worshiped in our land. These are the "religions" of choice. The wicked are found in what we call the churches. They are also found in our government, the banking and mortgage industries, and schools across this nation. They possess lying, blasphemous, greedy mouths.

False prophets abound. I joined a conference call of a well-known "prophet" a few years ago. At the end of the call, he asked how many minutes were on the call. When told it had been 23 minutes, he calculated the call cost to be $1,023.00. He then demanded the people on the call send in $23,100 to cover his costs!

Jeremiah 5 continues; *²⁶ "Among My people are the wicked who lie in wait like men who snare birds and like those who set traps to catch people. ²⁷ Like cages full of birds, their houses are full of deceit; they have become rich and powerful ²⁸ and have grown fat and sleek. Their evil deeds have no limit; they do not seek justice. They do not promote the case of the fatherless; they do not defend the just cause of the poor. ²⁹ Should I not punish them for this?" declares the LORD. "Should I not avenge Myself on such a nation as this? ³⁰ "A horrible and shocking thing has happened in the land: ³¹ The prophets prophesy lies, the priests rule by their own authority, and My people love it this way. But what will you do in the end?*

Hebrews 12:7-11 responds: *If you endure chastening, God deals with you as with sons; for what son is there whom a father does not chasten? But if you are without chastening, of which all have become partakers, then you are illegitimate and not sons. Furthermore, we have had human fathers who corrected us, and we paid them respect. Shall we not much more readily be in subjection to the Father of spirits and live? For they indeed for a few days chastened us as seemed best to them, but He for our profit, that we may be partakers of His holiness. Now no chastening seems to be joyful for the present, but painful; nevertheless, afterward it yields the peaceable fruit of righteousness to those who have been trained by it.*

So God is asking what we will do through this time of chastisement. Will we humble ourselves before the living God and repent? Will we stop living like the world, choosing instead to get our priorities in order? Will the dead in the pews wake up? Will the remnant rise up?

It is the remnant God is going to use to bring His kingdom plans and purposes to fruition to reach the masses. It is Holy Spirit filled and led prayers, coupled with the voice of the remnant, that God will use to bring about real and lasting change. We need to be on our faces, interceding for our nation, using the words of Jesus, *"Father, forgive them, for they do not know what they do"* **(Luke 23:34)**.

Jeremiah 31:34 states, *No more shall every man teach his neighbor, and every man his brother, saying, 'Know the LORD,' for they all shall know Me, from the least of them to the greatest of them, says the LORD. For I will forgive their iniquity, and their sin I will remember no more."*

May 30, 2011

Vision:

THE TRAP

The Spirit of the Lord is warning and warning. He has not released me yet. I pray you have been following the words the Lord has given these past few weeks; The Measuring Line in His Hand (Part 1, 2, 3), The Valley of Kidron Parts 1 & 2, Jeremiah 5...this morning, yet again, I received another word of warning:

The Lord showed me a vision. I saw what looked like a mountain cave concealed in shrubbery. I was standing in front looking at it when two huge hands and arms, composed of the greenery, branches and vines, formed and crossed the opening (as if one had crossed their arms across their chest). The arms then uncrossed and opened toward me, lying flat to create a ramp into the open cave.

I watched as people began to walk up the ramp into the mouth of the cave. They were saying, "Oh, it is the way to the Lord. He has come for us to take us out of this world. It is the rapture."

My grandson was scared, so he came and held My hand. I started walking up the ramp, intending to look at where these people were REALLY going, as I knew it was not the Lord. There was a check in my Spirit, so I turned and walked away.

As I watched from a distance, masses of people continued to enter the cave, never to be seen again. A small group of people gathered at the entrance trying to figure out where the people were really going, just as I had been doing.

Subsequently, these people out front and I found ourselves in a building. A man began to speak. I didn't see him, I just heard him. He was saying, "It was hard work, and a lot of it."

People began to talk to each other, wondering if they had made the wrong decision. They began to wonder aloud, "Maybe I should have gone with the others into the cave...Maybe we should have taken the easy way...Maybe we missed the Lord...Maybe it really was the 'rapture'..."

The Lord took me back to the mouth of the cave. He showed me that it was a camouflaged cage; a trap. Once people were in the trap, there was no way out. The "arms" of shrubbery had re-crossed and returned to covering the opening. The people were trapped in the cage (**Luke 21**: [34] "Be careful, or your hearts will be weighed down with carousing, drunkenness and the anxieties of life, and that day will close on you suddenly like a trap. [35] For it will come on all those who live on the face of the whole earth. [36] Be always on the watch, and pray that you may be able to escape all that is about to happen, and that you may be able to stand before the Son of Man.")

The people who were outside the cave represented the remnant. The laborers are few and the work is plenty. The cage represented the deception of the evil ones, masquerading as light encouraging people to compromise and take the easy way in their walk with the Lord. This is the broad road. Those who entered represented the ones whom the enemy holds in bondage; thinking they are serving the Lord, but not grounded in the word and lacking discernment. They were fooled by seducing lying spirits and not in a genuine, committed relationship with the Lord. They claim they know Him, but did not. This led them to be deceived and ensnared in the trap.

There are so many voices bombarding us from every angle. We need to make sure we know the voice of the Shepherd.

John 10:3 *To him the doorkeeper opens, and the sheep hear his voice; and he calls his own sheep by name and leads them out.*

John 10:27 *My sheep hear My voice, and I know them, and they follow Me.*

Lord give us eyes to see and ears to hear what the Spirit of the Lord is saying! Abba, Father, give us discernment! Do not let us follow the voice of another!

I hear the Lord exhorting us, "Be strong, My children, be strong. My Spirit lives inside you and He will lead you into all truth. Trust Him! Seek the fullness of Him. The Spirit was sent to be your helper, stop minimizing Him. Your trust in Him and your baptism by Him are key to your survival in the times ahead."

If you are not baptized by Holy Spirit seek the Lord for this!! We all *need* the fullness of God!! *I know the need for baptism of the Holy Spirit has fallen upon deaf ears!* I have preached it, I have encouraged it, and it does seem to fall on ears that cannot hear. I am sitting here crying, interceding with *such* a burden on My heart, pleading with you not to fear. The God of all goodness and grace would not give you an evil gift. God intends for us all to walk in the gifts of the Spirit, to further His kingdom. He intends to lead us safely through the maze of voices and dangers to our true home, safe with Him.

Jesus said it was better if He went home so the Father would send Holy Spirit. From My own testimony, I have lived with the Baptism of Holy Spirit and without; there is no comparison. My relationship with the Lord was minimal prior, compared with the depth of My relationship with the Lord after Holy Spirit "baptized" me in fullness.

Matthew 7:11: *If you then, being evil, know how to give good gifts to your children, how much more will your Father who is in heaven give good things to those who ask Him!*

John 14:26: *But the Helper, the Holy Spirit, whom the Father will send in My name, He will teach you all things, and bring to your remembrance all things that I said to you.*

June 4, 2011

JEREMIAH 6

Within a couple of days after the Lord had me release the word on Jeremiah 5, He led me to a section of Jeremiah 6. I never had the opportunity to write down what He showed me at that time, as everything that could possibly come into My life to distract me did, with errand after errand for Praising in the Park, a sick mom, sick grandkids, and work. Every day, Holy Spirit reminded me; Jeremiah 6, Jeremiah 6, Jeremiah 6!

Last night I worked until after midnight and then the Lord, again, referred me to Jeremiah 6. I read the chapter once more, but was too tired to write. Around 1:30 a.m., the Lord woke me with these words;

"My hand has risen against this nation. This people claim to know Me, claim Me as their own, yet their heart is far from Me. When they say peace, we shall have peace. They have no peace."

I was so tired, but grabbed a pen and pad, and after writing the above, I literally fell asleep with the pen in hand and paper on my lap. In the morning, I did not have the entire unpacking of this word, so as the Lord gives further revelation, I will add the updates.

I have been praying about the word, "North" in this chapter. Who is the enemy from the North? Every time I pray about this, all I see is the White House. Yes, the White House, but it is no secret this administration has not hidden the anti-Christian and anti-Israel agenda. I believe the Lord is showing me Jerusalem in this word represents the "Church" and this nation.

Jeremiah 6 - NKJV

Impending Destruction from the North

[1] *"O you children of Benjamin, Gather yourselves to flee from the midst of Jerusalem! Blow the trumpet in Tekoa, And set up a signal-fire in Beth Haccerem; For disaster appears out of the north, And great destruction.*

[2] *I have likened the daughter of Zion To a lovely and delicate woman.*

[3] *The shepherds with their flocks shall come to her. They shall pitch their tents against her all around. Each one shall pasture in his own place."*

[4] *" Prepare war against her; Arise, and let us go up at noon. Woe to us, for the day goes away, For the shadows of the evening are lengthening.*

[5] *Arise, and let us go by night, And let us destroy her palaces."* [6] *For thus has the LORD of hosts said: "Cut down trees, And build a mound against Jerusalem. This is the city to be punished. She is full of oppression in her midst.*

[7] *As a fountain wells up with water, So she wells up with her wickedness. Violence and plundering are heard in her. Before Me continually are grief and wounds.*

[8] *Be instructed, O Jerusalem, Lest My soul depart from you; Lest I make you desolate, A land not inhabited."*

[9] *Thus says the LORD of hosts: " They shall thoroughly glean as a vine the remnant of Israel; As a grape-gatherer, put your hand back into the branches.*

[10] *To whom shall I speak and give warning, That they may hear? Indeed their ear is uncircumcised, And they cannot give heed. Behold, the word of the LORD is a reproach to them; They have no delight in it.*

[11] *Therefore I am full of the fury of the LORD. I am weary of holding it in. " I will pour it out on the children outside, And on the assembly of young men together; For even the husband shall be taken with the wife, The aged with him who is full of days.*

[12] *And their houses shall be turned over to others, Fields and wives together; For I will stretch out My hand Against the inhabitants of the land," says the LORD.*

[13] *" Because from the least of them even to the greatest of them, Everyone is given to covetousness; And from the prophet even to the priest, Everyone deals falsely.*

[14] *They have also healed the hurt of My people slightly, Saying, 'Peace, peace!' When there is no peace.*

[15] *Were they ashamed when they had committed abomination? No! They were not at all ashamed; Nor did they know how to blush. Therefore they shall fall among those who fall; At the time I punish them, They shall be cast down," says the LORD.*

[16] *Thus says the LORD: "Stand in the ways and see, And ask for the old paths, where the good way is, And walk in it; Then you will find rest for your souls. But they said, 'We will not walk in it.'*

[17] *Also, I set watchmen over you, saying, ' Listen to the sound of the trumpet!' But they said, 'We will not listen.'*

[18] *Therefore hear, you nations, And know, O congregation, what is among them.*

[19] *Hear, O earth! Behold, I will certainly bring calamity on this people— The fruit of their thoughts, Because they have not heeded My words Nor My law, but rejected it.*

[20] *For what purpose to Me Comes frankincense from Sheba, And sweet cane from a far country? Your burnt offerings are not acceptable, Nor your sacrifices sweet to Me."*

21 Therefore thus says the LORD: " Behold, I will lay stumbling blocks before this people, And the fathers and the sons together shall fall on them. The neighbor and his friend shall perish."

22 Thus says the LORD: " Behold, a people comes from the north country, And a great nation will be raised from the farthest parts of the earth.

23 They will lay hold on bow and spear;They are cruel and have no mercy; Their voice roars like the sea; And they ride on horses, As men of war set in array against you, O daughter of Zion."

24 We have heard the report of it; Our hands grow feeble. Anguish has taken hold of us, Pain as of a woman in labor.

25 Do not go out into the field, Nor walk by the way. Because of the sword of the enemy, Fear is on every side.

26 O daughter of My people, Dress in sackcloth And roll about in ashes! Make mourning as for an only son, most bitter lamentation; For the plunderer will suddenly come upon us.

27 " I have set you as an assayer and a fortress among My people, That you may know and test their way.

28 They are all stubborn rebels, walking as slanderers. They are bronze and iron, They are all corrupters;

29 The bellows blow fiercely, The lead is consumed by the fire; The smelter refines in vain, For the wicked are not drawn off.

30 People will call them rejected silver, Because the LORD has rejected them."

The remnant of Israel in Jeremiah 6 represents the remnant of the true church. It represents the remnant of this nation in this word.

Things are moving rather quickly. The government will continue to increase their oppression and control on all the people, as well as the attacks on Christians and the true remnant church. The false church will continue to "evolve" and change with the political and anti-Christ environment.

We need to return to the godly foundations of this nation and the church. The church/nation needs to repent! We *must* stop the compromise and return to the ancient paths. We need to return to the basics; the unadulterated Word of God. Jesus is the Word, and there is power in Him.

Holy Spirit leads us in all truth. We need to focus on the basics; the virgin birth, the crucifixion, the blood of the lamb, and the resurrection. We are to be obedient and serve the Lord. We are to abide in Him. There we will find rest in the midst of chaos.

Religion will not save. Tradition will not save. Only relationship with the One, true God, will rescue souls, restore hearts, and renew minds. We have an assignment which we were born again to accomplish. The Lord has been speaking loudly and clearly to those who have eyes to see and ears to hear. He has sent the watchmen, and they are sounding the alarm.

June 11, 2011

Sermon:

JEREMIAH 2

We had an incredible night at Praising in the Park! Today I was exhausted and went upstairs to read the word and relax, hoping to take a nap. The Lord had other plans...

I had just sat down and reached for My Bible when the Lord spoke very clearly, "Jeremiah 2." I read it in the *King James Version*, *The Message*, the *New King James Version*, and the *New Living Translation*. What I read caused me to cry, both literally, and outwardly to the Lord to forgive the people, the church, and the nation, for they know not what they do, nor have done.

My heart is grieved to the core when I see what is going on in the world and how far and how fast this nation has drifted in recent years. That is heartbreaking enough, but the heartbreak escalated to a whole new level as I finished reading the words from the heart of God He has been giving from the other chapters in Jeremiah, and now this one. It is as if I can feel, through these scriptures, the very heart of God, breaking for his children. I am sobbing as I am writing this...

These scriptures also refer to Israel, but they paint a picture of the United States. Please read this chapter;

Jeremiah 2, New Living Translation (NLT)

The LORD's Case against His People

¹ The LORD gave me another message. He said, ² "Go and shout this message to Jerusalem. This is what the LORD says:

"I remember how eager you were to please me as a young bride long ago, how you loved me and followed me even through the barren wilderness.

³ In those days Israel was holy to the LORD, the first of his children. All who harmed his people were declared guilty, and disaster fell on them. I, the LORD, have spoken!"

⁴ Listen to the word of the LORD, people of Jacob—all you families of Israel! ⁵ This is what the LORD says:

"What did your ancestors find wrong with me that led them to stray so far from me? They worshiped worthless idols, only to become worthless themselves.

⁶ They did not ask, 'Where is the LORD who brought us safely out of Egypt and led us through the barren wilderness—a land of deserts and pits, a land of drought and death, where no one lives or even travels?'

⁷ "And when I brought you into a fruitful land to enjoy its bounty and goodness, you defiled My land and corrupted the possession I had promised you.

⁸ The priests did not ask, 'Where is the LORD?' Those who taught My word ignored me, the rulers turned against me, and the prophets spoke in the name of Baal, wasting their time on worthless idols.

⁹ Therefore, I will bring My case against you," says the LORD. "I will even bring charges against your children's children in the years to come.

¹⁰ "Go west and look in the land of Cyprus; go east and search through the land of Kedar. Has anyone ever heard of anything as strange as this?

¹¹ *Has any nation ever traded its gods for new ones, even though they are not gods at all? Yet My people have exchanged their glorious God for worthless idols!*

¹² *The heavens are shocked at such a thing and shrink back in horror and dismay," says the* LORD.

¹³ *"For My people have done two evil things: They have abandoned me—the fountain of living water. And they have dug for themselves cracked cisterns that can hold no water at all!*

The Results of Israel's Sin

¹⁴ *"Why has Israel become a slave? Why has he been carried away as plunder?*

¹⁵ *Strong lions have roared against him, and the land has been destroyed. The towns are now in ruins, and no one lives in them anymore.*

¹⁶ *Egyptians, marching from their cities of Memphis and Tahpanhes,have destroyed Israel's glory and power.*

¹⁷ *And you have brought this upon yourselves by rebelling against the* LORD *your God, even though he was leading you on the way!*

¹⁸ *"What have you gained by your alliances with Egypt and your covenants with Assyria? What good to you are the streams of the Nile or the waters of the Euphrates River?*

¹⁹ *Your wickedness will bring its own punishment. Your turning from me will shame you. You will see what an evil, bitter thing it is to abandon the* LORD *your God and not to fear him. I, the Lord, the* LORD *of Heaven's Armies, have spoken!*

²⁰ *"Long ago I broke the yoke that oppressed you and tore away the chains of your slavery, but still you said, 'I will not serve you.' On every hill and under every green tree, you have prostituted yourselves by bowing down to idols.*

²¹ *But I was the one who planted you, choosing a vine of the purest stock—the very best. How did you grow into this corrupt wild vine?*

²² *No amount of soap or lye can make you clean. I still see the stain of your guilt. I, the Sovereign LORD, have spoken!*

Israel, an Unfaithful Wife

²³ *"You say, 'That's not true! I haven't worshiped the images of Baal!' But how can you say that? Go and look in any valley in the land! Face the awful sins you have done. You are like a restless female camel desperately searching for a mate.*

²⁴ *You are like a wild donkey, sniffing the wind at mating time. Who can restrain her lust? Those who desire her don't need to search, for she goes running to them!*

²⁵ *When will you stop running? When will you stop panting after other gods? But you say, 'Save your breath. I'm in love with these foreign gods, and I can't stop loving them now!'*

²⁶ *"Israel is like a thief who feels shame only when he gets caught. They, their kings, officials, priests, and prophets—all are alike in this.*

²⁷ *To an image carved from a piece of wood they say, 'You are My father.' To an idol chiseled from a block of stone they say, 'You are My mother.' They turn their backs on me, but in times of trouble they cry out to me, 'Come and save us!'*

²⁸ *But why not call on these gods you have made? When trouble comes, let them save you if they can! For you have as many gods as there are towns in Judah.*

²⁹ *Why do you accuse me of doing wrong? You are the ones who have rebelled," says the LORD.*

³⁰ *"I have punished your children, but they did not respond to My discipline. You yourselves have killed your prophets as a lion kills its prey.*

31 "O My people, listen to the words of the LORD! Have I been like a desert to Israel? Have I been to them a land of darkness? Why then do My people say, 'At last we are free from God! We don't need him anymore!'

32 Does a young woman forget her jewelry? Does a bride hide her wedding dress? Yet for years on end My people have forgotten me.

33 "How you plot and scheme to win your lovers. Even an experienced prostitute could learn from you!

34 Your clothing is stained with the blood of the innocent and the poor, though you didn't catch them breaking into your houses!

35 And yet you say, 'I have done nothing wrong. Surely God isn't angry with me!' But now I will punish you severely because you claim you have not sinned.

36 First here, then there— you flit from one ally to another asking for help. But your new friends in Egypt will let you down, just as Assyria did before.

37 In despair, you will be led into exile with your hands on your heads, for the LORD has rejected the nations you trust. They will not help you at all.

There are obvious parallels between these scriptures and where we are as individuals, a church and a nation. Long ago the Lord broke the yoke of slavery with England and this nation was formed on a foundation of the living God. At one time we were a nation with the motto, *In God We Trust*, who actually believed those words; a nation abundantly blessed, and a light to the world. We were blessed with more than enough to be a blessing and the envy of the world. God's hand of protection covered us.

As a people, we have turned our back on God. As a church and a nation, we have been running after other gods; gods of self, movie stars, sports stars, rock stars, sex, money, and a government run by man to provide for our "needs." We have forgotten that God, Who created the Heavens and the Earth, provides for the government needs. We have abandoned our God for new idols, which are not gods at all. We have exchanged our glorious, omnipotent, omniscient, omnipresent God for worthless idols, filling the wells of living water with the dirt of selfishness and secular humanism. We have contaminated the river of God.

Instead of a leader among nations, we are becoming a follower. We have become a slave to oil producing countries. Our food and water are being bought up by big business in an effort to further control the people. Our cities, towns, and precious farm lands are drowning under flood waters. Winds have laid many towns in ruin. Sin, disobedience, and unholy alliances with enemy nations and governmental leaders have destroyed America's power and glory through rebellion. The LORD has rejected the nations we trust, and they do not help us at all.

When the disasters come – and the government abuses – we cry out, "How could this happen?" The answer is glaringly obvious. Yet, we deny, saying, "That's not true! I haven't worshiped the images of Baal!" and God queries as to how we can believe this, suggesting we go and look in any valley in the land, facing our awful sins. He says to the people in and out of the church *You are like a restless female camel desperately searching for a mate. You are like a wild donkey, sniffing the wind at mating time. Who can restrain her lust? Those who desire her don't need to search, for she goes running to them! When will you stop running? When will you stop panting after other gods? But you say, 'Save your breath. I'm in love with these foreign gods, and I can't stop loving them now!'*

We continue doing our own thing, thinking in all our manly wisdom that we know more than God. Like a thief who feels shame only when he gets caught, our governmental leaders, officials, priests, and prophets—all are alike in this; *To an image carved from a piece of wood they say, 'You are My father.' To an idol chiseled from a block of stone they say, 'You are My mother.' They turn their backs on God, but in times of trouble they cry out to Him, Come and save us!' But why not call on these gods you have made? When trouble comes, let them save you, if they can!* For you have as many gods as there are towns in America.

We accuse God of wrong doing when we are the ones who have rebelled. Our children have failed to respond to godly wisdom and discipline. The name of God and prayer have been removed from the schools and the public square. Abortion is birth control, embryos a science experiment. Murder, violence, and mayhem are entertainment. The church has killed the gifts and ministries of the Spirit as a lion kills its prey.

God has blessed us with every possible blessing, yet the people rejoice because they are free from God ~ filing lawsuits, demanding; crying out for tolerance for their ungodly sinful ways.

God says, "They do not extend the same cry for tolerance for My children who love Me and refuse to compromise My word. Presidents and leaders in the highest offices are disgracing their houses with fornication; glorifying other gods while removing Me from their midst, all the while claiming to know Me. Their hearts are far from Me. They rewrite My word to suit themselves, and create a god in their own image to avoid offending anyone. My message is offensive. My message is foolishness to those who do not believe. In all their foolishness, believing they are wise, their "wisdom" will be their destruction.

In the name of freedom from God, they believe they will be free. In reality, they fall deeper and deeper into bondage. They plot and they scheme the destruction of My children, the church, and this nation, behaving like a prostitute selling to the highest bidder, sacrificing innocent babies and the poor on the altar of mammon. They exchange honor and trust for money and sex, keeping people in bondage to the government rather than teaching them to stand on their own two feet with eyes on God as their provider.

People are silent as the blind steal, kill and destroy the very things that made the Church of Jesus Christ the "Church." They say it is good. Arrogance reigns supreme, but I am exposing. I am bringing those things, contrived in darkness, to light. I have been exposing the hidden agendas, adultery, and crimes against this nation. Who will restore honor and integrity to the church and this nation? I ask questions and continue to expose ~ to see what will you do. What will you do? What is the point where you will stop tolerating and exclaim, 'Enough is enough!' What side of the fence will you find yourself on?"

I hear the mantra from the people; God is not angry, He is a loving God. We tolerate sin in the church in the name of love and we say there is no consequence for sin. We believe that God is not angry that we remove the cross, the blood, the resurrection, Holy Spirit and His gifts from the body of Christ. The authority and power in the name of Jesus is denied, yet we insist, God is with us! We believe that we just need to find the right program to attract the people to our god. If we stuck with GOD'S program, we would not have a need for others.

Religion will not save. Tradition will not save. A relationship with the One true God saves. It renews hearts and minds. The Lord has been speaking loudly and clearly to those who have eyes to see and ears to hear. He has sent the watchmen who are sounding the alarm. It is what we were born to do...our purpose in Him, once born anew.

The signature scripture for Praising in the Park is **Psalm 26:12** in the *New Living Translation*. It states, *I have taken a stand and I* *will publicly praise the Lord.* We are here to do just that. Each of us must understand, there is no room for compromise. There is no room for apathy. We have been called for something greater than ourselves; a mighty work is waiting to be poured through each of us, which none of us fully sees or knows.

If you can see the battle rage around you, if you can feel that enemy of complacency and apathy overwhelm you, if you can hear the call of God and His army in the land getting louder and louder, then I invite you to stand before your God this day and pledge your allegiance to the lamb. Take up the sword of His Word, be obedient to what He asks you to do, and *know* that you have been chosen for such a time as this!

Tell Him, "I surrender! I raise a banner to Your name! I accept Your assignment, here I am, Lord send me!"

I hear the Lord saying;

"I am the Lord your God and I tell you this day, I LOVE my children and I do not desire any should be lost. I am sounding the alarm through my watchmen. Will you heed their call? To the one who kills the prophets and stones those who are sent to her, how often I wanted to gather your children together, as a hen gathers her brood under her wings, but you were not willing! You wanted no part of Me. Going your own way, doing your own thing, dancing with the god of this world. I am a jealous God and I want you all to Myself. Dance with Me, My children, dance with Me; follow My lead."

Who are you dancing with? The one true God, or the gods of this world who deceive and distract, lulling into a false sense of security? Are you serving a god created in your own image or do you have a real relationship with the Father? Are you still holding back and doing things your own way? The Lord is sounding the alarm, there is danger ahead. The lights are flashing, the railroad crossing is down. The siren is blaring; are you on the broad path? Now is the time to surrender to the Lord!

June 2011

Vision:

WALTZ AND THE WOLF

In a vision, I saw an ornate Victorian ballroom with gold leaf and chandeliers. People in formal attire from the 1920's were waltzing. It was a very nostalgic scene.

The scene changed to one of our military bases; I was there to visit my son. It soon became clear the base had been infiltrated by Islamic terrorists. They took me and several others hostage. There was a Muslim man, a soldier, who tried to help me, or he pretended to. They were forcing us all onto an airplane. I realized he really was not trying to help me, so I wrestled myself free and ran. As I was escaping, I realized he never tried to stop me. I knew if I had boarded the plane, I was finished.

The waltzing and nostalgia refers to the innocence of the past. People were enjoying themselves in a time of prosperity, but there was danger! The terrorist/enemy has gone undercover and was pretending to be a part of the military; our protection, our Government, helping, us, but in reality, lying in wait to destroy us/this nation. We were completely oblivious and the attack or bondage will come as a surprise. However, the Lord is exposing. We just need to adjust our spiritual eyesight. The problem now is that God *is* warning. He *is* exposing, but people are blind and deaf and do not care.

June 14, 2011

MY KINGDOM COMES IN ITS FULLNESS

I am the Lord your God and today I say, My kingdom comes in its fullness to the lives of My children ~ to walk as you have dreamed to walk. My faithful ones, who toil in My fields to bring in the harvest, the Lord your God speaks to you this day. My kingdom comes, My will be done on earth as it is in Heaven. The anointing to walk in the fullness of My Spirit falls from heaven as a thick oil rain.

What is coming you ask? The greatest move of the Holy Spirit the world has ever known. As the world gets darker, the Spirit burns brighter. As the moon pours forth to bring its light to the dark night, My light will pour through you to light the dark night of the soul. As darkness and calamity increase, My children who have gone through the correction of the Spirit will emerge victorious, unaffected by the darkness.

I give you eyes to see through the darkness as I did for the Israelites during the plague of darkness upon the land of Egypt. My children, you will see as if it was daylight, and you shall emerge from the darkness with the silver and the gold from those who have oppressed you and tried to keep you captive.

June 22, 2011

PROVISION IS IN THE FIELD

This came to me this morning while I was only half awake;

"Provision is in the field. When you are doing the work you have been called to do, you will find your provision, for I am the Lord your God and I will not leave you Fatherless. A loving Father provides for his children, and you are my child. Why are you worried? Why are you fretting? My eyes are upon you, My child. Stand. Stand in faith and see the salvation of the Lord."

J

June 26, 2011

THE LITTLE THINGS

I am the Lord your God, and you have an amazing and remarkable future. So many of My children are caught up doing the day to day activities of life. They think this is all there is. They think they have been forgotten. They think this is their future, more of the past.

Remember, I have said that if you are faithful in the little things, you will be trusted with more and bigger things. Child, be faithful in the small things of life, for I want to send the big things. There is much to do and the laborers are few. My kingdom plans and purposes have not changed. People have become too busy. They expected huge miracles. Expecting huge God assignments, they are not faithful or obedient to follow out My instructions for the small things in the kingdom.

Do not despise humble beginnings; they are character building in the lives of My children. Sometimes it is not a mighty move, but a series of smaller steps that get you where I am taking you; a lesson in obedience, a lesson in learning to hear My voice. If you are disobedient in one step, you are stalled on the path to where I am taking you. Fine tune your hearing. Listen for the voice of the Lord. Hearken unto My calling. Obey My instruction. This is the key to where you are going; to move you from where you are, to where I need you to be...Father God.

July 1, 2011

WHY GOD CHOSE YOU!

The day after the Lord had me preach about the fullness of the Spirit, He kept telling me His children need to come to Him as little children, in that wide eyed wonderment, to accept the gifts of the Spirit and to allow them to move through them.

We come to God, thinking from our religious stuffiness and pride that we do not need all the gifts the Lord said we need. Yet He intended for us to have them to empower us to minister to others. Mostly we are afraid we will look foolish. Children readily receive, wanting every gift their dad has to give them. Shouldn't we be the same? We need to understand clearly, God's ways are not our ways and just because we do not understand, makes it no less God. It actually makes it MORE God.

We make plans, we dream, we think we know better than God, but one thing I have learned in My walk with the Lord is He *never* does anything the way I think He should. Not how I think, when I think, why I think, or through whom I think. The end result is *always* better than what I thought it should be. How amazing and humbling God is.

The next time you think you know how it should be, remember what the scriptures tell us:

1. God chooses the foolish things to confound the wise.

2. God chooses the weak things to confound the strong.

3. God chooses the wretched things to humble the exalted.

4. God chooses the hated things to humble the dignified.

189

5. God chooses the things that are powerless to defeat the powerful.

When you mediate upon these things, you will understand why God has chosen you!

If you are one who has thought of every excuse possible for not giving your life to the Lord, or have made every excuse to not fully surrender to Him, even though you claim to be His child, no matter what the excuse, God does not look at things the way man does. God placed within you the criteria He was looking for, so that He could make you a powerful warrior in His kingdom.

What do you say? Are you ready to lay down the excuses and give your life back to the One who gives life; the One who allows you to take every breath, who holds your very heart in His hands? That God, who came to earth thinking of the depth of His love for you; who chose to die on a cross, pouring out His love to save us...The One who is right now making intercession for each of us in Heaven. Won't you receive His love and sacrifice? This is one of the few things in life that truly is a win–win situation.

July 19, 2011

SEE WITH YOUR HEART

I am the Lord your God, and today I say;

Repent, for the kingdom of God is at hand. It is much closer than many people think; complacent and living life like the world when My coming is on the horizon. I am the Lord your God and I am in control. I move the sun and moon and stars in their alignment. When you look at them, do you see Me in control of the heavens, or a cosmic explosion? It's all in your perspective. You will see Me in everything with your heart, not with your eyes.

I am just a thought away, in the big things and the small. I can be seen or not seen in all that is around you. You see with your eyes, but I want My children to see with their hearts, then you will see Me. You will hear Me speak; I speak in the roar of a wave and the tweet of a bird. I speak to the hearts of men, yet so many are deaf to My call. They are blind to My creation that screams, *I am the Lord your God. All that I am, everything that I have done, I have done for you.*

What will you do with Me, the Lord your God? Will you live for Me? Will you see the divine appointments? Will you see Me in the wind and the rain? If I orchestrated all of creation to sing My praise, what makes you think I am not orchestrating the things in your life to bring Me praise, to make your life a reflection of My glory in the earth? So, like the birds, the sea, the wind and the rain, when people see you, with their heart they will they see Me? Will they hear you praising My name?

July 20, 2011

Wheat and Tares

Matthew 13:24-30

The Parable of the Wheat and the Tares

24 Another parable He put forth to them, saying: "The kingdom of heaven is like a man who sowed good seed in his field; 25 but while men slept, his enemy came and sowed tares among the wheat and went his way. 26 But when the grain had sprouted and produced a crop, then the tares also appeared. 27 So the servants of the owner came and said to him, 'Sir, did you not sow good seed in your field? How then does it have tares?' 28 He said to them, 'An enemy has done this.' The servants said to him, 'Do you want us then to go and gather them up?' 29 But he said, 'No, lest while you gather up the tares you also uproot the wheat with them. 30 Let both grow together until the harvest, and at the time of harvest I will say to the reapers, "First gather together the tares and bind them in bundles to burn them, but gather the wheat into my barn."

Many people believe the wheat and the tares refer to the church and the world living together until the final harvest. It does, but it also refers to the wheat and the tares together within the church.

I always thought a tare was a weed, and some translations of this scripture say "weeds." Upon doing some research, I discovered that in bible times, the enemy would sow tares into the crops of God's people. A tare looks like wheat when it starts out, but as it matures, its appearance changes. It develops long "ears" and instead of a wheat kernel, it grows black poisonous kernels. In a sense, it is like a wolf in sheep's clothing; it starts off looking like a wheat, or genuine Christ follower, but turns into poison, deadly to churches and ministries, causing division and trying to take over the field and the church of God. I suppose the question should be, are we a wheat or a tare?

There is a remnant of true surrendered Christ followers who are seeking the heart of the Father, and there are those whose hearts are far from Him. They both call themselves Christians. Jesus said a good tree bears good fruit and a bad tree, bad fruit. In **Matthew 7:21 –23**: Jesus stated, *"Not everyone who says to Me, 'Lord, Lord,' shall enter the kingdom of heaven, but he who does the will of My Father in heaven. Many will say to Me in that day, 'Lord, Lord, have we not prophesied in Your name, cast out demons in Your name, and done many wonders in Your name?' And then I will declare to them, 'I never knew you; depart from Me, you who practice lawlessness!'*

Jesus had a lot to say to the religious leaders in His day. They looked like wheat, but in reality they were tares. They knew the words; they had head knowledge, but they did not have heart knowledge. They did not *know* the Lord; there was no relationship. Jesus had a lot to say to the religious leaders in His day, and He is saying the same thing today.

There are many wolves in sheep's clothing deceiving the sheep, but there are just as many vessels chosen by God to speak into the lives of His children. These leaders are not honored as having been hand selected by God, yet they continue to speak His truth.

We cannot be blessed as an individual or churches if we are undermining God's plans or God's chosen vessels. Jesus declared, *"If you have seen Me, you have seen the Father,"* (John 14:9). Just like the Pharisees, when we fail to see God in the vessel He has chosen to minister through, we are coming against the very God we claim to serve.

Jesus made it clear in His dealings with the religious leaders of His day, and it is no different today. Religion will not save you. It is a relationship with the Lord that will save you. Jesus said people had a form of godliness but deny His power. The gifts, the power and fire of the Holy Spirit that Jesus commanded the disciples to receive, is not felt to be necessary in much of Christendom today. In many churches there is no fresh rhema words of God.

God wants us yielded to the leading of the Holy Spirit at all times. He wants us hungry for all He has to give His children. He has so much more for us than many have been taught or experienced. Let this be our Isaiah moment; let it awaken us to the truth of His glory and power, that we, as he when catching a glimpse of the Holy God, cried out, *"Woe is me – for I have seen the Lord."* May we all get a glimpse of our Holy God that causes us to stop and reflect on our lives, to repent of what we need to repent, to confess what needs to be confessed, that we may consecrate ourselves daily.

God always honors humility. Praise the Lord He does not leave us where we are! Praise the Lord, He wants us to be a reflection of Himself! May we watch what we say and do that we might show Christ to the world. We do not want to find out too late that we are a tare and not wheat. It is far better to humble ourselves now, repenting and inviting Holy Spirit to change us. We want to hear, "Well done, good and faithful servant," (Matthew 25:21) not "Depart from Me, I never knew you" (Matthew 7:23).

Father, help us fine tune our spiritual eyes and ears. Let our hearts be soft and receptive. We ask that You give each of us an understanding of who we are in You, and what we are capable of doing for the kingdom when our eyes are on You and our hearts are in Your hands. Let us be the salt and the light in this dark world. May our touch be Your touch. May we see and hear as You see and hear. May our hearts be Your heart. Break our hearts daily for the things that break Yours. Help us to be real and transparent, that nothing will detract from You. Let Your love shine through us., in Jesus name, Amen.

July 26, 2011

FAVOR OF GOD

The favor of God is upon you, my child, walk like it. Stop living a defeated life when all of Heaven is available to you. Each one of my children is blessed and highly favored; you must fine tune your eyes and ears to hear what the Spirit of the Lord is speaking. If you can't hear my voice, or see the path, how can you obey my instruction? Each one of you is where you are today because of instructions ignored or obeyed.

I am speaking to my children all the time. Settle yourselves to hear from your Heavenly Father. The Spirit is your teacher and your guide. He is crucial to moving through the Kingdom. He is your warning to avoid a pitfall. He is your navigation system to obtain the blessing. He is the One who is your trail guide to keep you safe, warn of the pitfalls and keep you on the path of righteousness. He also will help you avoid the rabbit trails, quicksand, and traps of the enemy on the walk of life.

Do not ignore Holy Spirit. He is the one who will lead you safely home. Consider not the words of man. Consider the words in My book, left to you for guidance and direction, available to confirm these words. Man preaches things that are not of Me. Man preaches things that are of man. My word confirms what is truth. Do not fear the Spirit. Do not fear the gifts He has to give you. Do not fear what man will say or do to you. Open your arms wide and reach to the Heavens. Your God is provider of all things.

Man seeks to limit you, but a limitless God lives inside you. He will do great and mighty things that you know not at this time. Man has perverted My system. They have caused you to fear the helper. If you do not fear Me, if you do not fear My Son, why do you fear the Helper I sent? Man's reasoning is foolish, for he seeks to control you, to stifle Me within you. Cast off the wisdom of man as an old and dirty garment; put on My garment of truth and let your light shine among men, for the light of God is within you, waiting to burn brightly without being dimmed by a lamp shade. I am the light. The Son of God shines with the brilliance of the sun. Come out of hiding, My child.

Challenge the words of Pastors and leaders that do not line up with the truth of My word; those half-truths and words of man. Shine like the jewels you are; set My light free.

August 3, 2011

THE ENEMIES IN THE LAND

All is well, My child; the birds chirp and the sun shines. My hand is upon you, My child; the hand of blessing and favor. It may not look like you are blessed, it may not feel like you are blessed, but you are blessed and highly favored. Your Father, God, has spoken a reminder to you today.

Move in My power. Move in My spirit to affect change. Wherever you go, change the landscape. Claim the land of this nation for God, your Father. Joshua's, take the land for My name ~ take it back! It was given to you; a blessed land, an inheritance of My goodness and mercy, a land which I put My name upon for you. The land of Canaan is still there, take the land, Joshua's, I am giving it to you. Wherever your feet trod, claim the land for Me. Arise mighty warriors, arise in this hour, for the day of reckoning approaches. Fight the good fight; I have prepared the way.

The enemies in the land are the same enemies now, as then:

Canaaninites: Addictions, perversions, exaggerated people pleasing.

Hittites: Subliminal torments, phobias, terror, depression and deceit.

Amorites: Obsession with earthly fame and glory, domineering.

Perizzites: Limited vision, laziness, low esteem.

Hivites: Vision limited to enjoying earthly inheritance, hedonism.

Jebusites: Suppression of spiritual authority in fellow believers, legalism, apathy, fear and disappointment.

http://shamahelim.info/girgash.htm#The_7_types_of_evil_spirts

Another source lists them this way:

1. Hittites: Spirit of anger and violence

2. Girgashites: Spirit of idolatry

3. Amorites: Spirit of pride and boasting

4. Caananites: Spirit of depression

5. Perizzites: Spirit of apathy

6. Hivites: Spirit of control

7. Jebusites: Spirit of weariness

http://archive.org/stream/BreakingFreeFromBondage_784/BeingReleasedFromBondage_djvu.txt

The enemies have not changed. I have not changed. My children, many sleep rather than fight, and remain silent rather than speak. They are apathetic. Speak for your God who speaks through you. Fight for your God who is fighting for you. Let the God in you arise and shout the battle cry. Raise a banner for the world to see; I am your God and you are My children. The oceans may roar and the storms around you rage but you speak for Me. Peace, be still in you in your life. Remind the wind, the waves, and the storms of your life that your God lives! You are loved! The storms gather, the mountains tremble, time grows short. Look up; hear Me! Prepare the way of the Lord.

August 5, 2011

LAST CHANCE

I am giving the churches one last chance to stand before their God. Repent, for the Kingdom of God is at hand. Behold, it is in your midst. These are My houses, built to worship Me, and they are filled with man's wisdom and knowledge. I am unwelcome. I have to be there on their terms or so they think, but I left years ago. They did not know the God they claimed to serve, so they had no idea when I was gone. They keep man in and Me out. They are ivory towers where people are locked away and hidden; My power is denied.

August 6, 2011

REMNANT

Abba, our Father, your children, your remnant are crying out to you for this nation. This nation under God, in God we trust. There are more than 50, Abba. These are your people, we are here, we have eyes to see and ears to hear what you are saying! Sodom and Gomorrah, repent today before the living God! Hear our cries, oh Father, hear our cries for mercy on this nation, the church, and a people who have strayed.

Use each one of us to be change, to return to the ancient paths. Forgive the leaders, forgive this president, senate and congress, and our local governmental leaders. Forgive the pastors who have turned their backs on You. Who continue to use Your name, ignoring your wisdom, Word and Spirit, struggling in their own strength to run this nation and the churches. Their wisdom is foolishness compared to Yours. Help change our ways, to dismiss our wrong thoughts, our wrong desires, and our wrong actions as we raise our hearts to Heaven in surrender to the One true God. We ask forgiveness. Forgive us, for we know not what we do. How we have grieved Your heart.

Scrub us clean. Wash the government from the President on down to every local representative; include our churches, pastors, prophets, evangelists, elders, bishops, and every servant. Cleanse us in your blood. Forgive us our trespasses. We humble ourselves before You, the One True living and Holy God! Renew our passion, our fire, renew our minds today. Give us boldness to speak and to act as You have called us to do. Help us to take a stand and refuse to compromise Your word, to be single-minded, bound to the mind of Christ.

Forgive us for the times we have refused to obey. Give us Your heart, so we can *be* Your heart in our homes, churches, and cities. We are not seeking Your hand or face. We are seeking Your heart this day. You are the only One who can make a way. There seems to be no way out of the mess we have created in this nation through our arrogance, pride, and forsaking of You! We thank You for making the way. May all men *know* that it was *You and not man* who turned this around, for Your glory!

Your remnant is alive and well. We are contending for the future. We are contending for wells of fresh water. We are contending for souls! We are contending for your word to penetrate the hearts and the minds in this nation and in the church. As Your eyes search to and fro, we call out, "Here I am Lord, send me. Use me, equip me and speak through me. Let my hands and feet be your hands and feet. Let my eyes and ears be your eyes and ears." Let our hearts beat in unison with Yours, to be Your heart in this land. Let our breath be the breath of life in this world. We humble ourselves before You, the One true God, the God of all grace and mercy that we do not deserve. *FORGIVE US*, in Jesus Name; Amen and amen.

August 7, 2011

TEXAS DROUGHT AND THE NATION

Yesterday was the day of prayer and repentance, called by Governor Perry of Texas. I pray you participated and joined the chorus of praise, worship, repentance, and prayer that was lifted up across this nation. This was a God moment, I pray you kept the appointment.

As I was praying again this morning for the nation and the church, I asked the Lord to send the rain to the parched land. His response came quickly;

"Do not pray for rain. Pray that *My* people will prosper in the time of drought as Isaac did. He received no rain. He received no more water than his neighbors, but he prospered in the time of drought and ALL knew the God of Isaac was the *one true God*. All knew God was with him, as it was impossible that he would prosper 100 fold in the drought, '*but God*'."

This is not just a word for Texas but for all the remnant in the nation.

Genesis 26 (NKJV) *¹ There was a famine in the land, besides the first famine that was in the days of Abraham. And Isaac went to Abimelech king of the Philistines, in Gerar. ² Then the LORD appeared to him and said: "Do not go down to Egypt; live in the land of which I shall tell you. ³ Dwell in this land, and I will be with you and bless you; for to you and your descendants I give all these lands, and I will perform the oath which I swore to Abraham your father. ⁴ And I will make your descendants multiply as the stars of heaven; I will give to your descendants all these lands; and in your seed all the nations of the earth shall be blessed; ⁵ because Abraham obeyed My voice and kept My charge, My* *commandments, My statutes, and My laws."* ⁶ *So Isaac dwelt in Gerar* ¹² *Then Isaac sowed in that land, and reaped in the same year a hundredfold; and the LORD blessed him.* ¹³ *The man began to prosper, and continued prospering until he became very prosperous;* ¹⁴ *for he had possessions of flocks and possessions of herds and a great number of servants. So the Philistines envied him.*

God wants to show himself strong in the lives of his children. Trust Him. Put your faith in Him. He WILL make a way where there seems to be no way. He WILL show Himself mighty in the lives of his children. He WILL provide. Listen for His instructions; He will lead you through.

August 16, 2011

REAP

I woke up this morning hearing;

Ask the people, when will you reap what you sow? When will your selfishness catch up with you? When will your failure to give tithes and offerings catch up with you? When will your failure to help those placed in your path catch up with you? When will your disobedience, your failure to do what I have asked you to do, catch up with you? Be still and *know* that I am God. I am not man, that I can lie. Know what you reap, you have sown. In due time, your "harvest" shall come. What will *your* harvest be?

August 19, 2011

GIDEON

I watched the news this past week about the financial woes of the nation, which are affecting me personally as well as others I know.

As I prayed over all the prayer requests from the ministry, I kept hearing and seeing **Romans 8:22**; *For we know that the whole creation groans and labors with birth pangs together until now. All of creation is groaning.*

<u>The Message Bible</u> says it this way; *22-24All around us we observe a pregnant creation. The difficult times of pain throughout the world are simply birth pangs. But it's not only around us; it's within us. The Spirit of God is arousing us within. We're also feeling the birth pangs. These sterile and barren bodies of ours are yearning for full deliverance.*

We are birthing a move of God. As I was led to preach recently, we are contending for anointing, gifts and mantles that the Lord will empower His people with, which will bring light into the darkness of the land and usher in the King of Glory. At the same time, judgment is coming on the land, if it's not already here. The fiscal irresponsibility, disobedience, and rebellion to the Lord has caught up to this nation. The remnant is crying out for mercy, while too many continue to barrel down a path of destruction.

As **Romans 1:20** clearly points out, "*For since the creation of the world, God's invisible qualities—his eternal power and divine nature—have been clearly seen, being understood from what has been made, so that people are without excuse.* The people are without excuse. God has made Himself manifest all around, and still people do not believe. Many came face to face with Jesus and did not know who He was, including those religious leaders who should have known.

These past few days, the Lord has been speaking to me, and through others, about Gideon. I know I will preach on this in greater detail at some point, but I feel led to share it now in brief. When the economy tanked in 2008, my business went from busy and regular work to nothing for almost a year. Then, I began to receive contracts again, although not enough. I was just able to pay the pressing bills; yet there was nothing left over. These past few months I had begun to feel some hope again that things were finally going to turn around for the better.

I had been busy ministering to people and invited to preach. We had people coming up for prayer, deliverance, repentance, and healing; powerful things, then, BAM...Bad news. Doom and gloom in the economy and suddenly I am back to square one with no work coming in. I know with everything in me that God is my provider; not my business, nor the ministry, but truth be told, I am frustrated and weary. Has anyone else been in this place?

Gideon and the Israelites planted their seeds, as I planted my seeds. They believed a harvest was coming. I, too, believed after all the hard times and hard work, the harvest was coming. But then the Midianites came in like locusts to steal the harvest. Gideon and the people, just like me and many of you, thought they were going to be blessed and that things were going to turn around. Instead, the enemy came in like locusts and stole the harvest. In a similar place, we are feeling left with little to nothing and are wondering why.

The word of the Lord is this;

You are also a mighty man or a woman of valor, as the angel said to Gideon. You have not understood why things seem to be going backwards from where you thought you were going.

When it was time for battle the Midianites had about 150,000 troops. The Lord instructed Gideon to send home those who were afraid and did not want to be there. God then pared them down further by how they drank water from the river. He reduced Gideon's army down from 75,000 to only 300, which makes no sense in the natural. God reduced the troops, so that when they had the victory, no *man* could boast.

God is paring down and pruning the "armies." He is removing those whom we thought were going with us, those whom we thought had our backs. He is removing our resources; the things and people we counted upon, so that we cannot boast when *He* brings the victory.

God next instructed Gideon to give each man a torch in a clay jar and a trumpet, and instructed them to march into battle. When the men reached the enemy camp, they blew the 300 trumpets and broke the jars that contained the torches. Each of the 300 men had a torch, and when the enemy saw them coming, they thought each torch represented 1000 men, as was the case in those days, which meant they were outnumbered 2 to 1. When the men heard the trumpets and saw the torches they ran. Some turned on one another.

The torch in the earthen jar represents the Holy Spirit in us! They broke the earthen jars, as we need to break our pride and our flesh; our need to do things by our own strength. We need to stand up in these times and obey the strategy of the Lord in order to win the battle and claim our harvest. God had the victory in a way that seemed to make no sense in the natural; the same is true for us.

We do not need more people with us. We need to step back and realize it's not by our might; we need to break our pride and let Holy Spirit shine through us, remembering it is *not by might, nor by power, but by His Spirit* (**Zechariah 4:6**). It is by His wisdom.

We have a part to play. We need to trust and obey the Lord to bring the victory. God will multiply the few who stand with us, as well as the resources we have, to confuse and confound our enemy. God will not share His glory with anyone.

Was that for anybody else, or was it just for me?

As we come before the Lord, I feel led to ask you to humble yourself and lift up a prayer for the nation, the church, and those who claim to know the Lord but their hearts are far from Him. Cry out for mercy. God is always about restoration; He gives grace to the humble. Pray that our nation would garner a glimpse of the Almighty. Pray for the people in the church who are dead in the pews to be resurrected by the power of Jesus. Seek strategy from the Lord, that we may be victorious in the battles we are facing. Pray that we will most assuredly *know* it is by His Spirit that we are victorious.

Romans 8:19 *For the creation waits in eager expectation for the children of God to be revealed.*

We are birthing a move of God. We are contending for mantles, anointing, and gifts and to be light in a dark and scary world. As with Gideon, I pray the Lord gives you a revelation that you are a mighty man or woman of valor. Like Esther, may you know that you have been handpicked by God for *such a time as this*!

August 25, 2011

WARRIOR WOMEN

I endue you with power to accomplish those things you did not think you would accomplish...A revelation from the Most High God, your Father, to His faithful daughters.

The Lord your God sees your pain, sees the hurts you have suffered in your fight for the kingdom. Mighty Deborah's who have stood in faith, going toe to toe with the enemy when the men surrounding you refused to step up and take their rightful place. You knew my plans going forth were more important than fear. There was no negotiation. When the men said "no," you said "yes, Lord." I have risen up mighty warrior women who dared to go with the power of God where they were told they could not go. Where you were told women should not go, you have fought and contended for your future, your families, and for the men in your life who refused to fight. You have been found faithful to stand before Me, your God.

You seek Me; you sought Me when all was against you. You stood, wielding your weapons, and you will receive your just reward for keeping the kingdom moving forward in faith. Virtuous women, mighty women of valor, all of Heaven calls you blessed. My beloved, beautiful women, it is going to be okay. Your children will be okay. Trust in the Lord your God. How could I let down My faithful?

All is well, mighty warriors, all is well. When the water rises and the fire burns, you are surrounded by My presence. My love envelopes you just as the warmth of the noonday sun floods through your windows on a cold day. Mighty women of valor, you are My beloved. My hand is upon you to do great and mighty things. The enemies who have tried to shut you up, tried to limit and oppress you, will find themselves on the other side, their tables turned. As Esther stood and prayed, then saw her deliverance and that of her people. She turned the tables on Haman through faithful obedience. So will you. Those who have sought to destroy you will realize they have touched the apple of My eye ~ My bride, My beloved, the ones whom I love. They will dread the day, for they will reap what they have sown. As what Haman created to destroy was used against him, so too, the very plans concocted in secret against you will be exposed in the light. Tables will be turned. The Lord your God has spoken daughters of the Most High, give Him praise!

REVELATION 3: TO MY TRUE CHURCH

Since last October the majority of the prophetic words the Lord has had me release basically say the same thing. If we break it down into the simplest terms it is something like this;

Tell His children, to stop living like the world. Stop looking like the world. Stop talking like the world. Stop behaving like the world and focus on Him. The Lord is shaking everything that can be shaken, until all that will remain is that which is founded upon the rock of Jesus, Amen?

The Lord has told us repeatedly, in word after word, that the *only* safe place to be is in Him...abiding, living, breathing; wholly surrendered to Him. He has promised that if we do that, He will safely bring his true children through. Out of His great love for us, God is warning of what is to come if we do not pray and repent. He does nothing without speaking it through the prophets and His words are always meant to bring about restoration and blessing.

The Lord has spoken to us about the judgment to come on the nation and her church. We know that God relented in His word when people repented and turned back to him, and I pray this happens in our nation. The remnant has been crying out for change. The Lord has called His Joshua's to rise up and take back the land, the church, and the nation. We were a promised land, and enemies have risen up against God, Himself, within our boundaries. He spoke to us about David, reminding us that we are not the runt of the litter. To the contrary, we are mighty warriors in the Spirit. There are many weary warriors in the natural, myself included. We are warned not to become weary in well doing, but it can be tough at times. I, like many of you, have felt the weariness in this season. It seems like we are going backwards. The resources are dwindling, the people we thought were going with us are gone. The enemy has come in like locusts and stolen during what we thought was going to be a time of blessing and harvest.

Last week the Lord gave us a brief word about Gideon to remind us that we are mighty men and women of valor, hand chosen by God Himself for such a time as this. God is pruning, He is decreasing the things we have been depending upon so that when the victory comes, no man can boast. No man will be able to take credit. Victory will come to pass, even though it looks impossible in the natural as we are outnumbered and out resourced. The Lord wants us to understand that we will win; not by *our* strength or wisdom, but by the wisdom, strategy, and power of His Spirit.

This week the Lord spoke Revelation Chapter 3 to me. This is a word that ought to fill you with excitement. It is a word that is not just for the end time, but for us here and now, from the heart of Our Lord. It is given to His true faithful children, for such a time as this.

Revelation 3:7 *"And to the angel of the church in Philadelphia write: 'These things says He who is holy, He who is true, "He who has the key of David, He who opens and no one shuts, and shuts and no one opens": ⁸ "I know your works. See, I have set before you an open door, and no one can shut it; for you have a little strength, have kept My word, and have not denied My name. ⁹ Indeed I will make those of the synagogue of Satan, who say they are Jews and are not, but lie—indeed I will make them come and worship before your feet, and to know that I have loved you. ¹⁰ Because you have kept My command to persevere, I also will keep you from the hour of trial which shall come upon the whole world, to test those who dwell on the earth. ¹¹ Behold, I am coming quickly! Hold fast what you have, that no one may take your crown. ¹² He who overcomes, I* *will make him a pillar in the temple of My God, and he shall go out no more. I will write on him the name of My God and the name of the city of My God, the New Jerusalem, which comes down out of heaven from My God. And I will write on him My new name. ¹³ "He who has an ear, let him hear what the Spirit says to the churches."'*

That excites me! As I said, it is not just a word for the future return of the Lord, but it is for us here and now. It is for this coming judgment that the Lord has warned is on the horizon if our nation and the church do not repent.

The Lord is calling for he who has an ear to hear what His Spirit is saying. He is telling us that He knows our works, and that He has set before us an open door that no one can shut. Even though it looks like the doors are being slammed in your face at every turn, God has set before us open doors that NO ONE ~ no man, no evil plan of the enemy ~ can shut. Praise Him!!

I believe God is saying that He is not through with us yet, we still have an open door. He knows we are running on little strength, so many are weary from the constant battle these past few years, but He knows we have kept His word...that we have NOT denied His name. We have been faithful to His word, and refused to compromise. For those of us whom this rings true, He will make those enemies who claimed to be believers but were workers of iniquity, those who claimed to be our friends but lied to and cursed us, those who have persecuted the God in us, to come and bless us because they came against Him. He will make sure that all will know that the Lord God almighty loves each of us, and that we are His children. He will protect us from anything or anyone who would dare raise their hand against us. It will be as if someone touched His very eye if they touch you or I, and because we have kept His command to persevere, He also will keep us from the hour of trial which shall come to test those who dwell on the earth.

So as in all those prophetic words the Lord has spoken these past months, He is confirming the only safe place is covered by His blood, abiding in the shadow of His wings. The only safe place is living in surrendered obedience to the Lord God as we fight the battle by his Spirit. Amen? Let's give the Lord a praise for His word!

September 1, 2011

WALK ON RAGING SEAS

I am the Lord your God, and today I say;

This is the first day of the rest of your life. Stop living in the past. Stop thinking like the past, stop living as old wineskins and move on in Me. Shake off the restraints the enemy has used to hold you back and keep you in bondage, for I died so that you can be free, free in Me, free of your yesterdays and possessing hope for your tomorrows; free of the bondage of man, living in victory. The storms may rage around you, but I am in the midst of them. Look at Me; I promise you will walk atop the raging, storm-tossed sea.

Faith is a mainstay. Faith is the key to opening doors and calming the raging sea. Faith in Me when you can feel Me not. Faith when you can't see Me and are blinded by the trials and storms of life. Faith when you cannot see the shore.

When it feels unsafe, I am there with you. I knew everything in advance that would befall you; the big and the small. I knew the decisions you would make and where you would end up. I knew you would heed My call and choose life, and life more abundant. Your Father is with you in the big and the small. Continue to choose life.

September 21, 2011

SOUND OF THUNDER

Yesterday, the Lord began to speak to me about Elijah. He said there was a drought in the land for years, and we as a nation have been in a drought for 3 years. God told Elijah to present himself to Ahab, and He would send rain. God is asking us to present ourselves to Him in a "new" way, His way as in the days of Elijah, and He will send the rain.

"Hear the sound of thunder. Hear the sound of an abundance of rain; a time of cleansing. A God-appointed time approaches in the Spirit. Will you yield your flesh to meet Me on My time frame, *My* timeline? For I hear the sound of thunder, I hear the sound of an abundance of rain for those who push back the darkness, for those who do it My way, I will bless. I give instructions this day for you to follow.

You have been crying out for breakthrough; I am offering you the key. My Word never changes. What I ordained was not just for yesterday, nor just for some of My children, but for *all* My children. Do not worry what man will think. I have an appointed time; a process in place to heal you and see you made whole, to see those stubborn issues dissolve before your very eyes, to see breakthrough and deliverance. Come, take My hand as we journey together to do a new thing, which is of old, to bring you deliverance and inner healing once and for all. I have come to set you free. Meet with Me. I have set an appointment to meet with you".

October 1, 2011

RELEASE

I was awakened at 1:18 a.m. and remained awake until 3:30 a.m. The Lord spoke this to me;

I send My prophets to speak, to uncover the mysteries. They bring light into darkness and calm to chaos. I am the Lord, your God, who pleases you. I am the God who covers you. I am the God who has you. Receive your healing; My gift to you this day. I want to bless My children. I want you to choose life! Let Me release you from the baggage you carry around, showing you the mercy and love of the Father, for My love is great. My mercy is unending with you, My child, go in peace.

October 3, 2011

ENLARGING YOUR TERRITORY

I am enlarging your territory. I am giving you the land in conjunction with My word. There will be breakthrough. Lives are about to change in My kingdom. Living for the moment, with no thought to the future, life will change.

October 4, 2011

TAKE

As I was sitting in church last Wednesday, the Lord directed my attention to the offering buckets being passed and how few actually give. I heard the words. "So many take and take and never contribute to the expenses of My house."

Last night the Lord woke me from a SOUND sleep with this word; He just kept repeating the first few words until I became coherent and grabbed a pen and paper...

"If I call upon each one of you to take out what I place in your hand, can I trust you to use it for My kingdom purposes? So much stealing of what belongs to Me. It is used for selfish gain and not sown into the kingdom, then you wonder why there is no harvest and why you can't get a break. You failed the test. Can I trust you, or not?

October 6, 2011

SHAKING

Hold on! I am not done shaking. There is more to come. Then there will be a time of national choice. Declare prayer and fasting one week before the election.

I am the Lord your God. So many of My children are looking this way and that. They have taken their eyes off of Me as their provider and the author and the finisher of their faith. They are letting their flesh take over, trying to manipulate and force things to happen rather than look to Me and wait on Me. I want the very best for My children, not second best; not to settle for anything less. So many are settling out of fear.

My love, My child, you are the apple of My eye. You know how to give good gifts to your children, how much more do I desire to give *My* very best to you. I never promised your life would be easy, though I know the TV preachers have. The truth is, you are blessed going in and coming out, but blessings and favor always comes with a price. My blessing and favor does not always look like man's definition of blessing and favor.

There were some who lived to see fulfillment of the blessings, others who did not because it came in a later generation. You do not understand. It is not just about you. Your faithfulness or lack of it affects not just you, but those around you, as well as those in future generations. Everything you do not obey requires a massive shift in the lives around you; a repositioning to allow another the chance to obey that same instruction. There can be lots of delays on the road to your future, depending upon your willingness to obey.

I choose to use people. Fine tune your hearing through the noise pollution so you can better hear My voice and obey. Hear and obey; an instruction missed is a blessing denied.

October 7, 2011

FAITHFUL

I am the Lord your God. Today I say, well done good and faithful servant. Faithful to stand when others failed to stand, when they fell to temptations of this world. Faithful to seek Me as the sun rises. Faithful to obey, unafraid to do the hard things. Faithful to show My love and share My message.

Your reward is in Heaven. I know things are tough right now, but do not lose heart. I am faithful to sustain you and meet your every need. Look to Me, I will never leave you or forsake you. I am the Lord your God and I am great and mighty. You are more than your circumstances. Creativity is flowing from My altar to My children. Listen for the sound of thunder and My still small voice ~ for My instructions to bring you into your future. Do not lose heart. I am with you, My child, in the big and the small, in the mighty and the mundane.

October 8, 2011

BLESSING SEEKERS

A Word for Yom Kippur (The Day of Atonement)

Seek and you shall find Me. Knock and the door shall be opened. Seek Me on My terms, not your own, for there is a way that looks right to man, but it is the way of destruction. Too many only want Me on their terms. Too many tell Me what and how they want things done.

My ways are higher than their ways, and the Lord your God knows best. Stop telling Me what to do, or how and when you will do it. Do as I ask, for I want the very best for you. Stop doing works of man or what you think I like. Simply do what I ask. Offer a drink to one in need. Show love, honor, and respect to one another. Point the way to Me, in word and deed; stop posturing and positioning yourself as if you are the greatest in the kingdom. Stop lording over the people, for the finest in the kingdom is the greatest servant of all. This tenet has been forgotten; it is not popular. I have watched pastors and leaders become kings of their kingdoms, rather than servants of all. Humble yourselves and wash the feet of My children; do unto the least of these. Things are backwards from how I intended. The Lord your God has spoken.

Even My children are in rebellion. Watchmen who talk without love; pastors are controlled by Jezebel. Counterfeit signs, disguised as My signs, wonders, and miracles, New Age and the occult have invaded My church. People are running from conference to conference for a spiritual high, rather than spending time in My presence. Worship teams play for their own glory, rather than mine.

Current economic trials are not just about money, they are to expose the heart of man and his true motives. Can you trust Me in the good as well as the bad times? So many, who's hearts remained far from Me, have walked away. They were here for wrong reasons, as blessing seekers, not God seekers; always seeking My hand and what I could give, never My heart.

Every day is an opportunity for change. What you choose to do, or not do, is a reflection of your heart. Do you reflect the heart of God, or the heart of man? Will you lay your heart on the altar? Will you lay it all down at My feet? No excuses. No rationalizations. No justifications. No control. No ultimatums. No conditions. The time has come to seek Me; to worship Me, not for what I can give, not for what you can get, but for no other reason than I AM!

THE ROOT OF BITTERNESS

The root of bitterness in your lives needs to be removed and exposed. Shovelful by shovelful, every hurt and place of unforgiveness needs to be dug up, overturned, and healed; removed at the root. Allow Me to do that work within you. Shovel by shovel, word by word, memory by memory, we will remove the dirt and expose the root. Then I will remove the source; not just cut it off, but dig it out and remove it completely. Come away with Me to the secret place, be willing to meet with Me in total surrender.

Sleep in Me. Sleep in My arms, child. I long to bring you comfort. The world is dark and scary, but you carry My light within you. It is designed to reach nations. Let your light shine through the dark night, exposing the works of darkness. Authority is increasing within you. The enemy will flee like a cockroach exposed to the light. I send you out, a sheep among wolves, be as wise as a serpent and harmless as a dove.

October 16, 2011

GO IN PEACE

Go in peace, My child. Stop stressing. Stop striving. I am the Lord your God and I promised to work all things for good for those who love Me. If you believe Me, trust Me to do just that. The striving and stressing is a symptom of a lack of trust, a lack of faith. There comes a point where knowing what is right is translated into action. Faith means action, not passivity. Faith is a decision. Trust is confidence.

Will you choose to trust Me, leaning not on your own understanding when things are confusing, when you cannot see the forest for the trees, when the path you have been comfortably on takes a detour, or becomes obscured by foliage? Will you yet trust when the wind blows, or the storm washes away the bridge across the river?

I can make a way where there seems to be no way. I can make My light shine in the darkest of nights and lead you home. Trust Me, My child, I am hope...I am your anchor.

October 19, 2011

HEART OF MY HEART

A revelation of who you are in Me; you are My child. You are My love, My joy, the heart of My very being. I gave Myself in death, that you might be free. No greater love is there than this...Heart of My heart, My very being resides within you.

October 2011

SUBTLE DECEPTIONS

Yesterday, I read the title of a post on Facebook® about a ministry luring Jews by advertising "supernatural conferences," then at the end telling them it was Jesus who was the healer. I did not give it much thought at the time, as I was busy with work, but this morning during my prayer time, the Lord began to speak to me about that.

He reminded me of other ministries that go to coffee shops and street fairs, setting up tables, attracting people with signs pointing to the supernatural such as dream interpretation and the prophetic. There is no mention of God until *maybe* the end of the interaction. I never thought too much about this, either, until this morning.

The Lord reminded me about these things, then posed this question. "Does the end justify the means?" The thought crossed my mind; better to get them saved any way possible...but then I settled on my answer. "*No*, the end does not justify the means."

The Lord continued, "I never deceived anyone nor did My apostles. People may have come to see signs and wonders, or hear Me speak, but they all knew who I was, whether they thought I was a Rabbi, or a prophet, they knew I represented God, even if they did not want to admit it. Even the ones who accused Me of casting out demons by Satan knew who I claimed to be." My mind went to Paul preaching about the "unknown" God. The Lord, knowing my thoughts, responded, "He used what they had, he did not deceive them."

He told me that by doing the above, people are attracting those who hunger for the supernatural, whether it is through Him, new age or the occult. When they see those signs, or approach the table seeking the supernatural, they are not thinking of God. They consider unholy things such as the occult and new age "wisdom." When and if, they are presented with the Truth, they end up believing, through this brief encounter, that the only way to get more of the supernatural is to make a profession of faith. Rather than helping these people understand that the point is not to get more of the supernatural, but more of God by coming to an intimate knowledge of Him, rather than seek supernatural manifestations. The majority end up off track and out of focus from the beginning. There is no follow up and no discipleship. What we have been seeing are people chasing signs and wonders; seeking God's "glory" by going from conference to conference. The Word tells us that *signs and wonders will follow us as believers*. We are not to follow the signs and wonders!

God continued His questioning, "Do you see the subtle and not so subtle differences? Do you believe the end justifies the means? It does not. I have never deceived anyone, I have never minimized Myself. My disciples never minimized Me, and I never forced myself upon anyone. It would be like you putting on a large crusade meeting and not putting your contact information in the advertising. It is ME who draws them. People need to make a choice on a platform of truth, to come to Me or not. They need not believe that they were led to Me under false pretenses. The enemy's subtle deception is everywhere."

This revelation has me grieved and I am in tears right now. My heart hurts. All I could say was Father forgive them, for they know not what they do. Lord, help us! Oh, Lord, have mercy! Set us on the true narrow road that leads to You. Open our eyes to truth!

COUNTERFEIT

I woke up to the Lord *asking* me if I wanted a word from Him this morning...

I thought, why ask me? Of course I do! He has never asked me that before, but when I came to the end of transcribing the word, I realized that the reason He asked was because this is a hard word. Everyone loves to give blessings and feel good encouragement...the question comes, will we still be obedient when it is a hard word?

You are My love, My gift to those around you. A gift of a reflection of My presence. A storehouse of My word. A revelation of My glory in a fallen world. I long to use you to point the way to Me in greater and greater manifestations of My Spirit moving upon the earth.

Will My people rise up? I am the real deal. Will My people rise up, claim, activate, and stir up the gifts within them? Will they be a vessel I can pour My glory through, a walking, breathing, demonstration of My glory upon the earth? So many are desperate to see Me move, to see signs and wonders, but they cannot differentiate the true from the false...they make a spectacle of themselves and bring harm, disparaging the kingdom and the gifts and the power of the God. Well-intentioned, desperate for more of Me, they lack discernment, looking to man rather than the one true God. To God be all glory, not man.

Seek and you shall find, ask, and the door will be opened. I withhold nothing good from, My children, and I am not withholding My power. Freely you receive, freely give. Do not look to the counterfeit. Do not look to the past. Look to Me, the giver of life, and you will see My glory working in you. I send My watchmen to warn.

So few listen, content in their cocoons of manmade religion, insulated from the world, but also from Me. Surrounded by half-truths and grave clothes, deaf to My call, they cannot hear from Me. I am calling you forth into the light of My true presence; the light of My truth. The light of My truth is found in My word. It abounds in *Me*, not the words of man.

When did you read that I or My disciples barked like dogs or got drunk? We did not; we remained sober-minded (**Titus 2:6, 1 Peter 4:7**). You did read of fits and strange behaviors in those with demons. Today in the church, it is backwards. The behaviors I wrote about in My word were demonic, but now accepted as manifestation of My Spirit. This is NOT My truth. No, My Spirit is joy, peace, love, and patience, not bizarre behaviors. It is My Spirit that sets the bizarre behaviors, the things that are wrong, back to normalcy. I am not the author of confusion. I declared that drunkenness is not a part of My kingdom (**Galatians 5:21, Luke 21:34**), so why would "drunkenness in the Spirit" be acceptable to me?

I am a God of order, not disorder. You are in danger, My child, of not inheriting the kingdom of God. You have been deceived into thinking what is wrong, is right. Be sober minded, be diligent, be hearers and doers of My word. Listen to that still small voice, the voice of discernment within you, and do not be deceived.

Cut the ties with the unholy. Fear God, not man. Cut the ties that bind to a system I left long ago. Do not be content with the counterfeit, a form of godliness, yet a perversion of My truths. My houses have become a mockery, void of My presence; so quick to accept the false as truth, and the counterfeit as more real than the reality I intended.

My presence is available to those who seek Me, to those who hunger after Me. Power, signs, wonders, and miracles from My very hand are available; a display of My glory in the land. There is no lack, there is fullness. There is no need to settle for less than My fullness.

What the early church had is available to you. I am no respecter of persons. They paid a price for the anointing. People today do not want to pay the price. I am not withholding from you. To whom is given much, much is required. Do not settle; wait upon Me in expectation and I will show up with all My power and glory. It will draw people to My presence in you.

Many do not want to hear what the Spirit of the Lord is speaking. Some will be convicted, others will lash out at the messengers. Many will not want to seek Me for truth, remaining content with the lies.

A word today to My children...Heed the message, for time is short. I do not want you on the outside looking in, wondering what has happened. Seek Me in Spirit and in truth. Turn, for the Kingdom of God is at hand.

October 26, 2011

RIGHTLY DIVIDE

I give you My sight to see all that is around you. I give you this day, My ears to hear what is around you. Activate My gifts within you, as many are blind and deaf to the spiritual things and the battles raging around you. You do not wrestle with flesh and blood, even though it feels like that at times. You must learn to see beyond the natural. Learn to listen for My voice in all things as I protect you from danger and the ungodly happenings around you.

Pick up your weapons and fight. Do not be afraid to fight the injustices you see. See through My eyes. You are not going alone to the battle. You are not going alone to speak. You are going at the prompt and leading of My Spirit. Feel the Spirit stirring as He rises within you.

You have a battle to fight; a Goliath who reared its ugly head, a mountain that needs to be moved. There are veils that need to be torn down to receive and release more of My presence within you. Whose are you? What will you hold on to? The Spirit in you, or doctrines and words of man? It is time to choose which side of the fence you will be on; the pure unadulterated Word, My Son, led by My Spirit in all things, or the words of man, intermingled with the words of your God, so as to lead you astray.

There is only one road that leads to life and it is much more narrow than many believe or choose to accept. It is time to get back to the uncorrupted Word of God. Put your trust in Me, not in horses and chariots. Drink from the pure spring that flows forth living water. Be pleasing and righteous before God and man, but refuse to "please" man, as this leads to compromise. I did not come to bring peace, but a sword; the sword of righteousness, the sword of the Word, rightly dividing and exposing truth, setting right the hearts of men.

October 2011

SEEMS TOLERANCE IS MISTAKEN FOR LOVE

My heart aches. The Lord in his mercy has been having me speak out boldly this past year, but even more so since July. Judgment is coming. It's here. The Lord sent me to preach a message to a church this past July. He told me that He was sending me to bring repentance to His house. They raved about how good the message was, but did not pay attention. He sent me back there with another message a couple of months later, to prophecy judgment for their rebellion and failure to repent. I watched as judgment fell upon that church. As of now, the spring of 2013, the church is closing.

My heart was broken. I cried and interceded from the minute the Lord revealed the message I was to preach. I spoke what He told me to speak. I could feel a tangible anointing, the people expressed how much the message moved them, how strong the Holy Spirit was, but there was no change. The warning unheeded. Judgment followed.

As the Lord conveyed in the previous word, *Subtle Deceptions*, and in the words *Counterfeit* and *Rightly Divide*, He is exposing all. He is not exposing out of accusation or condemnation, as so many express, but out of love. He desires to warn his children that we are in danger. Instead of taking it before the Lord, examining one's self, ministry, and church against the light of His Word, people lash out at the messenger, thinking it is I speaking against people. That is not the intent; I, just like other messengers, am responsible before the Lord to deliver the word He tells me to give.

Before I get a word to release, the Lord deals with me first. I have been in many of the very ministries, using some of the same methods of ministering, years ago. The Lord brought conviction to me, and is now having me speak His heart about those very same things I was a part of; if not an active part, at a minimum, my silence condoned.

I am not Holy Spirit to convict and make changes. I am just a messenger. Attacking the messenger is backwards. We have a responsibility to take all things before the Lord and examine ourselves, especially if it is uncomfortable and convicting. God is a God of love and restoration. He hates compromise and despises HIS holy name being used for unholy purposes.

Many people accuse me and other messengers of all sorts of things, speaking, "You're not in love, you are in fear, you hate people." They do not know me very well. and they do not know my heart is broken day in and day out over these very things; over these messages of judgment, warning, and correction. I, too, much prefer a warm fuzzy word. The Lord has spoken many of those, too. He asked me once, "Will you be a Daniel and obey Me, speaking what I will give you to speak, no matter how hard, and no matter who I call you to speak to?

I had a decision to make; either serve God wholeheartedly, or not. I believe that was a crossroad in My life. I believe we all get to that crossroad at some point. Over the past few years, as the Lord has been growing this gift, He has put a boldness in me to speak these words that, frankly, must be all Him and very little of me. Ask anyone who *knew me when*...I find myself asking too often, "Did I say that?" I laugh, because I don't recognize myself LOL.

The Jesus, Paul, James and Peter I read about in the scriptures were pretty darn bold and blunt; people were insulted. These men spoke the hard truth to all they met, and *that*, my friends, is real love! Real love is not lies, compromise, or distortion to keep the peace. No one accused Jesus or His apostles of not walking in love. If they came and spoke some of the very same words in our midst today, I am sure they, too. would be accused of not being in love. They spoke harshly; "Broods of vipers, get behind me Satan, Hypocrites!" Jesus took a whip and ran out the money changers; the profiteers in the church who were taking advantage of the people! Jesus did not do and say these things to the world at large, He did, and said them to the church of the day.

The above, plus some scriptures documented below, I have not been able to get out of my mind for months now. Paul voiced in **1 Corinthians 5:1**;

It is actually reported that there is sexual immorality among you, and of a kind that even pagans do not tolerate: A man is sleeping with his father's wife. ² And you are proud! Shouldn't you rather have gone into mourning and have put out of your fellowship the man who has been doing this? ³ For My part, even though I am not physically present, I am with you in spirit. As one who is present with you in this way, I have already passed judgment in the name of our Lord Jesus on the one who has been doing this. ⁴ So when you are assembled and I am with you in spirit, and the power of our Lord Jesus is present, ⁵ hand this man over to Satan for the destruction of the flesh, so that his spirit may be saved on the day of the Lord. ⁶ Your boasting is not good. Don't you know that a little yeast leavens the whole batch of dough? ⁷ Get rid of the old yeast, so that you may be a new unleavened batch—as you really are. For Christ, our Passover lamb has been sacrificed. ⁸ Therefore let us keep the Festival, not with the old bread leavened with malice and wickedness, but with the unleavened bread of sincerity and truth. ⁹ I wrote to you in My letter not to associate with sexually immoral people ¹⁰ not at all meaning the people of this world who are immoral, or the greedy and swindlers, or idolaters. In that case you would have to leave this world. ¹¹ But now I am writing to you that you must not associate with anyone who claims to be a brother or sister but is sexually immoral or greedy, an idolater or slanderer, a drunkard or swindler. Do not even eat with such people. 12 What business is it of mine to judge those outside the church? Are you not to judge those inside? 13 God will judge those outside. Expel the wicked person from among you.

Wow! We are *not* to judge *outsiders*; those who are outside of the church, the ones we tend to think it is okay to judge, we are not to judge, but the ones we think it is not okay to judge we are called to evaluate.

The other scripture I can't seem to shake is **Matthew 7:21-23**;

21 "Not everyone who says to me, 'Lord, Lord,' will enter the kingdom of heaven, but only the one who does the will of My Father who is in heaven. 22 Many will say to me on that day, 'Lord, Lord, did we not prophesy in your name and in your name drive out demons and in your name perform many miracles?' 23 Then I will tell them plainly, 'I never knew you. Away from me, you evildoers!'

It seems to me that tolerance is mistaken for love in the church and the world...Silence, in the name of "love." The problem is that we condone the happenings inside our church walls which, according to the Word, grieve the heart of our Father.

Jesus did not come to bring peace into the world. He came to bring a sword on which both sides are sharp. He is love, but also a consuming fire. He brings salvation, but He will also bring judgment. That is why I believe the Lord is having me share a *"What Did Jesus Really Say?"* series. I have posted scripture with the words of Jesus and people have gotten angry, accusing me of being hateful, but these are not *my* words. The gospel has become so perverted that people do not even recognize the words of the God they claim to serve. They point fingers and say "stop judging" when isn't that exactly what they are doing? They should be "judging based on the Word of God as the final authority, not the ways of the world.

It is long past time to examine ourselves, our God walk, our God talk, our hearts against the meat of the Word, separating the wheat from the tares that have been growing in our hearts and minds. In many cases, we have blindly accepted lies as truth and come into agreement with them, continuing to perpetuate them and even mislead others.

I am not writing any of this to vindicate myself, I would not even try to do that. I am sure many will disagree and attack me over this; you may argue on, but this is what God has laid on My heart for months, and this is what He is doing in my life and ministry. I believe, with all my heart, that this message is what is on His heart for His children. This is HIS message for us to hear and respond. I have been hearing similar messages being spoken by several others who are also going through these attacks; the Spirit of the Lord is speaking.

This IS a message of love! God loves his children. In his mercy, He has been speaking *REPEATED* warnings, and it is *ALL* about His love and desire for reconciliation and restoration. It is out this love He points out where we have missed the mark; not to accuse, attack, or condemn, but to restore. THIS IS LOVE!

The Lord has shown me, we should not be bragging about our love for others, or even our love for Him, because we do not know, nor can we know *anything* about real love without Jesus in us. Even then we fall far short. Many are being manipulated by Jezebels, and are manipulating in the name of love. That "love" is used to control so people can make a name for themselves, or build a ministry. It is not pointing to the God, Who Is Love.

October 27, 2011

TELL THEM WITHOUT CEASING

I am the Lord your God. I am in the midst of all you say and do. The King of Kings and Lord of Lords is your guide to life eternal. All that you ask in My name is yours. Stand in faith. Align your thoughts with My word and watch miracles happen. It is because of My good news and grace, as your loving heavenly Father, I pour out My goodness and mercy to a dark and thirsty world. They see Me not, but I am all around them. My beauty surrounds them, but they ignore Me.

Keep up the good fight of faith, weary warriors. Unite and find refreshment, and strength in Me. My goodness and My mercy, My grace is extended towards a world that is hurting and does not know the way home. Tell them without ceasing in word and deed, of My goodness and mercy. Cease not in the sharing of My love and grace unending, for time is short, and they perish every day without knowing Me.

Some are in rebellion; love them. Some are wounded and haunted by past wounds and deeds; love them. Some are living on the fence and in compromise; bring them to Me. Point the way to Me, remind them of Me. Cry out for mercy, for a lost and stubborn generation to return to the Lord their God, while there is still time, while I can be found. I will show them rest.

October 31, 2011

SHUT THEIR MOUTHS

Changes are coming to the economy and political arenas. Great upheavals are on the horizon, but I have not forsaken My children. I will sustain them with My right hand. All that you thought would be, and all that was, will be but a distant memory. However, I am the Lord, your God and provider. I will make a way where there seems to be no way; I will light a fire and direct you home. Gasoline prices will rise, powers will shift, upheavals will continue. The world is realigning; My purposes will be played out.

There will be great light that cuts through the darkness. The light of My spirit to enlighten hearts and minds, while others, blind and deaf, continue to stumble around in darkness. They are gods of their own worlds, masters of none. Instant destruction will be upon them. Be that vessel of light in the darkness. Do not be afraid to speak. How will they know if you do not speak? How will they hear truth through the abundance of lies? Speak My child, speak. You are responsible to speak, they are responsible to hear. It's all a matter of pride.

Witchcraft is prevalent in My church, done with intention, practiced without; cursing My children from the pulpit and in secret. Just like Balaam, I will shut their mouths. When they try and curse they will bless. I will shut the mouths of the lions and Jezebels who rise up against you. When they rise, they rise against My Spirit in you. They rise against My mighty right hand. They will not prevail.

My children, you are blessed. Rise up, call yourselves blessed, and move. Move through the obstacles; the mountains, and Goliaths that have risen up against you. My angels will lead you, as they led Lot out of Sodom and Gomorrah. The sword of the Lord is in your mouth. Speak, My child, speak. You have the power to speak life and death into your situations and all those around you. Speak to the mountains. Speak to Goliath. Goliath was defeated the minute David said, I will fight you in the name of My God. He rose up while others cowered in fear.

Those who have risen up against you; the mountains, Goliaths, and the lions who roar, are the doors to your next level in me. Rise up and fight in the name of the Lord, or choose to cower in fear. The decision is yours, but the battle is already won when you elect to fight in the name of your God.

November 1, 2011

I Long To Heal

I long to heal your heart, if you would only let Me. The past is a barrier to your future. It is like having a noose around your neck, then wondering why you can't take a full breath. I long to set My children free, free in Me, free in Me! Free of the past hurts and pains that you carry around and own. Hurts that settled in your Spirit, and the enemy tightened his noose ever so slowly till you were trapped; in bondage to his evil plans to choke your soul. He cannot have you, My child, but his presence can bind you and rob the fullness of your future in Me. Shake off the past. Close the doors to the sins and words spoken over you in the past.

The enemy worked hard to destroy many of you early, through sexual sins and abuse at a young age, but I long for you to be free; truly free, receiving the gift of freedom that I died to provide for you. I can heal you, I will heal it all. Bringing all things hidden to light, I delight to heal you Shine the light into your soul and the demons will flee. Silence can give them license to remain. Speak those things you have kept hidden, bring them to light, and the radiance of My presence will set you free. Forgive yourself, as I have forgiven you. Forgive others, so you will be forgiven, a circle of life will begin, bringing change to your situations. You will be amazed at the depth of oppression and torment that many of you have carried around. Freedom is calling out to you.

Won't you place your hand in mine? My intention is never to cause you more pain; I deliver you from it. Rise up, face Goliath in My name; he will go down. Just as that strategic stone hit the Goliath of old, My presence will drive yours to the ground, cutting off its head ~ the root of your pain. No more taunts, no more torment, no more fear, for the giant that dared raise himself against you will be defeated.

Trust Me to heal those hurts and pains you have buried deep within you. Bring them to My illumination that I might bring healing. My hand reaches out to you now. Take My hand, My child. The God Who loves *you* is reaching out, longing to heal your heart. When your heart is healed, your body will follow suit, for I am the Lord your God, and I desire to see you well. I died to cover you with My healing blood. Trust Me, My child, trust the Lord your God. I only have your best interest at heart. I bid you Shalom. Shabbot Shalom; nothing missing, nothing broken in your life. Speak it over yourself. Nothing missing, nothing broken, for I am the Lord. I am able and willing.

November 1, 2011

THE HARD TRUTH

I love you, My children. Many have been obedient and faithful, even when times were hard. You did what I asked you to do, giving no thought to the consequences or backlash. You have quickly sought to forgive the hurts and pain. You have not lashed out, demonstrating My mercy.

I commanded you to speak hard truth, in love to My children who are so deceived by the enemy. Yes, I am a God of love, but I am also a God of justice and truth. The enemy seeks to appease, to keep the peace at all costs, but I did not come to bring peace. I came with a sword, a love to purify the hearts and the minds of those who have fully surrendered to Me, choosing to serve Me in the good times as well as the hard times. To you who have eyes to see and ears to hear, the watchman speaks again...seek Me, seek My truth.

My presence will cost you something. To some it will cost all. Every one of My servants has paid a price for the anointing and power. Being My true follower costs; there is a high price to be paid. Many of you have willingly paid the price, and will continue to do so until I call you home. Others have never paid a price, being double minded and unstable in all your ways, taking the path of least resistance to keep the peace, proclaiming love to the exclusion of truth.

My love does not pacify, it purifies like fire. It is truth, burning through the chaff to reveal if a heart is completely mine. When your words seek to keep the peace, to make everyone happy, then My word has been compromised. It would not have been love if I had told the sinners I encountered that it was okay to continue in their sins. I told them, "Go, and sin no more."

I challenged and confronted the religious leaders of the day. It would not have been love to do otherwise. I spoke truth, and that truth hurt. It exposed their hearts, a two edged sword that brings freedom or a snare. To keep silent when you know a brother is sinning is not love. Love speaks with the intention to reinstate, not condemn. Mercy seeks return to relationship. Grace seeks to restore, not to hide or condone.

The Lord your God has spoken to His children, this day. Heed the message. Refuse to compromise My word. Live it out in spirit and in truth, seeking to restore to Me those who have wandered off the path of righteousness. There are many wolves in sheep's clothing who are subtly trying to deceive My children in word and deed. A little compromise here, a little compromise there. Speak truth with the goal of restoration, not alienation. Some of those who decry love and criticize freedom from religion are in a trap, mistaking manipulation for love.

I sent you as sheep among wolves. Listen to My voice, train your ear to hear through the distractions, discerning those among you. Not everyone who says to Me, "Lord, Lord" is My child. Look no further than the polls. There is only a small minority who admit they do not know me, yet if everyone who said they knew Me, did, the world would be a far different place.

November 4, 2011

IT STARTS WITH YOU

I am the Lord your God and I declare, today is the first day of the rest of your life. Shake off all the enemy has placed on you. Shake off what he has tried to use to defeat and silence you. Look to Me afresh. Break it off! Break it off, you are not what he has said! You are not crippled, you are not sick, you are not sad or depressed; you are blessed and highly favored, walking in My kingdom blessings. Shake free!

November 7, 2011

BLANKET OF LOVE

Let the peace of God surround you like a warm blanket. Snuggle into My presence as I envelope you in My love. How I long to spend time with My children. So many are so busy, missing out on My fullness. Draw Me close to you. I am the God of your todays and your tomorrows.

Behold, I make all things new. Stand in faith through the transitions. Stand through the hard times, for I am a faithful God, and I will never leave you nor forsake you. Lean not on your own understanding. Know that I am in the midst of all, and I am well able to bring you through.

November 11, 2011

MY PRESENCE REMOVED

I am the Lord your God. Judgment has begun in My house. You will see it expand as it spreads across the cities and the nation. All churches not found on the rock will be destroyed. They may still look like they are standing and open for business but all that is not of Me will be destroyed. My presence will be removed. Like a piece of spoiled meat they shall continue stinking and spewing foul gases; the last to know that I am not with them, I have left the premises. They will be the last to realize their dirge has played.

They will re-create themselves, haughty and self-righteous; centers for gatherings where My words have been compromised and twisted for the glory and benefit of man, leading many astray. Churches are filled; a wake of dead men's bones, as life has sucked them dry. They are dehydrated for lack of freshwater; the living water My presence and Spirit brings.

Give glory to your God in the highest, for He reigns. Shout out to the people, God reigns! God will bring the dead bones of your soul to life, re-creating you in perfection under the blood of the Son! The Spirit of God wants to reign in your heart! Come, all who are heavy laden, and be made whole. Rest from striving, for My burden is light.

Will you recognize Me when I come? The Pharisees did not, just as many religious leaders do not recognize Me today. I am the God of Abraham, Isaac, and Jacob. I am not the God of Ishmael. Turn from your wicked ways. Blood is on your hands, the blood of My precious children who trust too much, being led like sheep to the slaughter. I am the shepherd! I am the truth! I am the life.

There can be no substitute.

November 13, 2011

FREEDOM RINGS

I got into bed last night, settled in, and then heard...*Freedom Rings! Freedom Rings!*

Freedom rings! Declare the captives free from self-imposed and man imposed bondage. Declare freedom from slavery and the bonds of sin, for I have come to set you free! Declare the captives free; free in Me! The liberty bell is ringing.

Shake it off, shake it off, shake it off! Shake off all that is not of Me. Drop it like a hot potato, those sins in your life, those words spoken over you, those mindsets in conflict with Me. Declare your liberty.

I am the God who set you free. The prison doors are open. When will you walk free? It is not the prison doors that keep you there; the spiritual earthquakes of this past season shook your prison to the core and the doors flung open, but you choose to stay locked in a prison of your own making. Step out the doors and into the light.

November 18, 2011

DO NOT LEAN

I have been working far too many hours the past couple of weeks. When I awoke this morning, I just needed to hear from the Lord. I asked Him, what is the word for the day? Instantly, this followed;

Trust Me and do *not* lean on your own understanding. Your word for today, from the heart of your Father, is to trust Me and do not lean on your own understanding. So many of My children set off to "find" more of Me, but instead get caught up in subtle and not so subtle attempts by the enemy to lead them astray. My word gets twisted, half-truths spewed. I am in the little things just as much as I am in the big things.

There is no need to run from ministry to ministry, looking for more of Me. I am right here! When you spend time in My presence, you will find what you have been searching for all along. Keep it simple. Seek Me. Praise, worship, and talk to Me. Let your heavenly language speak what is on My heart for you, and you will find what you have been seeking; more of Me.

Draw close to Me, and I will draw close to you. I am not withholding anything from you. You cannot seek man to find more of Me; there are no short cuts.

Psalm 34

¹ I will praise the LORD at all times. I will constantly speak his praises

.² I will boast only in the LORD; let all who are helpless take heart

.³ Come, let us tell of the LORD's greatness; let us exalt his name together.

⁴ *I prayed to the LORD, and he answered me. He freed me from all My fears.*

⁵ *Those who look to him for help will be radiant with joy; no shadow of shame will darken their faces*

.⁶ In My desperation I prayed, and the LORD listened; he saved me from all My troubles

.⁷ For the angel of the LORD is a guard; he surrounds and defends all who fear him.

⁸ *Taste and see that the LORD is good. Oh, the joys of those who take refuge in him.*

⁹ *Fear the LORD, you his godly people, for those who fear him will have all they need.*

¹⁰ *Even strong young lions sometimes go hungry, but those who trust in the LORD will lack no good thing*

.¹¹ Come, My children, and listen to me, and I will teach you to fear the LORD

.¹² Does anyone want to live a life that is long and prosperous?

¹³ *Then keep your tongue from speaking evil and your lips from telling lies!*

¹⁴ *Turn away from evil and do good. Search for peace, and work to maintain it.*

¹⁵ *The eyes of the LORD watch over those who do right; his ears are open to their cries for help.*

¹⁶ *But the LORD turns his face against those who do evil; he will erase their memory from the earth*

.¹⁷ The LORD hears his people when they call to him for help. He rescues them from all their troubles.

^{18} The L ORD is close to the brokenhearted; he rescues those whose spirits are crushed.

^{19} The righteous person faces many troubles, but the L ORD comes to the rescue each time.

^{20} For the L ORD protects the bones of the righteous; not one of them is broken!

^{21} Calamity will surely overtake the wicked, and those who hate the righteous will be punished.

^{22} But the L ORD will redeem those who serve him. No one who takes refuge in him will be condemned.

November 20, 2011

CRY MERCY

I am Who I am. I am the same God yesterday, today and forever. So why do you fret? I was more than enough to deliver the children of Israel from captivity into the promised land. I was more than enough to provide for Isaac in the midst of famine. I was more than enough to fill the cruses of oil and flour for the widow women, and I am more than enough to provide for you.

Cry out church, *"Lord have mercy,"* for judgment starts in the house of God. My body is sick and wounded. My children are malnourished for My word has been diluted and compromised. I am calling you home, back to Me, the one true God. Stop living in lack; lack of My word, lack of My revelation, lack of My presence, lack of My power, lack of My healings and miracles. Stop living like the world.

Turn to the uncompromised word of God, that the church will be called the "Church Triumphant;" a beacon of light in the darkness, to call My children home. The famine of My word and presence will have passed.

Call out, *"God have mercy!"* I want to bring My children home; not to a place of complacency, but to a place of power. The loud voices of unity, crying out in the wilderness of My world, *"God have mercy."* Cry out from the depths of your souls, for judgment has come on the hearts of the people and they have been found wanting.

The true church is in labor, ready to be birthed again, to do a new thing, which once was an old thing...Usher Me in. Usher My presence in to a dry and thirsty land. If My presence arrives too quickly, it will run off the land, as the ground is hard. Till the land, prepare the fallow ground for righteousness in My Spirit. You will soon see what you long to see. In the midst of great darkness, My Spirit will shine as a light to nations, drawing them to Me.

November 27, 2011

LISTEN, CHURCH

I am the Lord your God, and today I declare, warn My people of the judgment.

Set aside all that is not of Me. Do not mix with the world and its ways, for My pure church has become a mix of everything unholy. My "church" has been defiled with the doctrines of man and the doctrines of demons. My children cannot see the truth from the lies and the counterfeit.

Rise up from among her, those who have eyes to see, and ears to hear what the Spirit of the Lord is saying to the church. Rise up from among her and flee the false signs and wonders. Flee the false Christ and the false doctrines of demons; return to the pure unadulterated word and church.

Cleanse yourselves, for you have been defiled. Cast away all that is not of Me. Come, stand before Me as My pure and spotless bride. Cast down the lies and the doctrines of man. Return to My holy Word, a holy way of living.

No, My grace does not cover willful and wanton sin. The day of reckoning is coming. I am coming in the clouds, in all My glory. Every eye will see Me, and every knee will bow before Me.

Listen "church," you have been found wanting, leading My children astray. You teach the doctrines of demons and man, *not* My pure, Holy Word. I am watching. As in the days of Noah, so shall it be. Which side of the ark door will you find yourself on? The only safety is in Me; in My blood. The only protection, in the shadow of My wings. Run to your God in heaven, not the gods of this world, for I am where your safety lies, both in this world and in the next.

May God have mercy. Say it. May God have mercy on My soul. All that is not founded on the solid rock is rubble, unstable, without foundation, unsuitable for building upon...foundations are crumbling and in disrepair.

Come back to Me, all you who are heavy laden, and I will give you My rest and set you on a firm foundation. The scales have been assembled. I am holding them in My hand. The church is in compromise. Churches perpetuating doctrines of demons have been found wanting.

Examine yourselves, examine your church, come out from among the harlot. What does light have in common with darkness? What should a child who calls himself Mine have to do with compromise of My word and false signs and wonders? Nothing! Nothing at all! Flee to the safety of the Rock of Ages.

Do not say, "Oh, this does not apply to me," for there is little that the enemy has not perverted in the world. There is little that has not been twisted from the pulpits of this world, for the benefit of man and the enemy's agendas. Man-made doctrines and doctrines of demons abound. Do not be deceived. Do you hear the alarm? Do you feel the tension in the air?

Now is the time to examine yourselves; stand before Me, naked and vulnerable. Allow Holy Spirit to show you truth. I am your God who loves you. Turn from among the compromise and flee to Me. I will lead you with all truth. Come to Me, you who are heavy laden, and I will give you rest. My burden is light, put down the loads you have been carrying. They are not of Me. The enemy heaps upon you to discourage and distract.

I want you free from bondage. A pure and spotless bride; the wedding feast has been prepared. I am issuing a warning to this generation of believers. You are in danger. Will you choose to fellowship with man or ME?

November 30, 2011

IS THIS FOR YOU?

I am not sure who this is for;

I woke to these words...You have been afraid of Me (God) all your life. I am the Lord your God and today I say this;

I am the Lord your God, why do you run from Me? Why don't you seek intimacy with Me? I am not the angry father who waits to punish his children. I am a loving Father. Everything good in your life comes from My hands. I am not looking to punish, I am looking to share My Son ~ My Life, with you; life eternal, enveloped in My love.

Won't you come to Me? I am not scary. I am love; love eternal. I am love which you cannot experience in life without Me. All of your life, you have been in fear of Me. All your life, you have been looking for love. I have waited patiently. Now I speak to you.

Hear My voice., *KNOW* this is for YOU. Do not hesitate, My arms are open, waiting to make all your hurts and pains disappear, waiting to reconcile your past to Me; I yearn to heal your heart, and move you into your future. The desires of your heart are not dead; they come alive in Me.

December 13, 2011

TITLE HOLDERS

I was praying about what was in store for 2012, and the Lord stated, **Jeremiah 3:23**;

Our worship of idols on the hills and our religious orgies on the mountains are a delusion. Only in the Lord our God will Israel ever find salvation.

As in past words, Israel refers to Israel, the United States and the Church.

I thought, "Lord, this is tough, a tough word." He impressed upon me that Jeremiah had to deliver this same word, and Daniel had to speak to the leaders of his day, so I was to speak, as it had risen up to Him as a stench.

Then the Lord spoke again, **Jeremiah 23**;

The Righteous Descendant

¹ What sorrow awaits the leaders of My people—the shepherds of My sheep—for they have destroyed and scattered the very ones they were expected to care for," says the Lord. ² Therefore, this is what the Lord, the God of Israel, says to these shepherds: "Instead of caring for My flock and leading them to safety, you have deserted them and driven them to destruction. Now I will pour out judgment on you for the evil you have done to them. ³ But I will gather together the remnant of My flock from the countries where I have driven them. I will bring them back to their own sheepfold, and they will be fruitful and increase in number. ⁴ Then I will appoint responsible shepherds who will care for them, and they will never be afraid again. Not a single one will be lost or missing. I, the Lord have spoken! ⁵ "For the time is coming," says the Lord, "when I will raise up a righteous descendant from King David's line. He will be a King who rules with wisdom. He will do what is just and right throughout the and. ⁶ And this will be his name: 'The Lord Is Our Righteousness.' In that day Judah will be saved, and Israel will live in safety. ⁷ "In that day," says the Lord, "when people are taking an oath, they will no longer say, 'As surely as the Lord lives, who rescued the people of Israel from the land of Egypt.' ⁸ Instead, they will say, 'As surely as the Lord lives, who brought the people of Israel back to their own land from the land of the north and from all the countries to which he had exiled them.' Then they will live in their own land."

Judgment on False Prophets

⁹ My heart is broken because of the false prophets, and My bones tremble. I stagger like a drunkard, like someone overcome by wine, because of the holy words the Lord has spoken against them. ¹⁰ For the land is full of adultery, and it lies under a curse. The land itself is in mourning— its wilderness pastures are dried up. For they all do evil and abuse what power they have. ¹¹ "Even the priests and prophets are ungodly, wicked men. I have seen their despicable acts right here in My own Temple," says the Lord. ¹² "Therefore, the paths they take will become slippery. They will be chased through the dark, and there they will fall. For I will bring disaster upon them at the time fixed for their punishment. I, the Lord, have spoken! ¹³ "I saw that the prophets of Samaria were terribly evil, for they prophesied in the name of Baal and led My people of Israel into sin. ¹⁴ But now I see that the prophets of Jerusalem are even worse! They commit adultery and love dishonesty. They encourage those who are doing evil so that no one turns away from their sins. These prophets are as wicked as the people of Sodom and Gomorrah once were."

¹⁵ Therefore, this is what the Lord of Heaven's Armies says concerning the prophets: "I will feed them with bitterness and give them poison to drink. For it is because of Jerusalem's prophets that

wickedness has filled this land." ¹⁶ *This is what the Lord of Heaven's Armies says to his people:*

"Do not listen to these prophets when they prophesy to you, filling you with futile hopes. They are making up everything they say. They do not speak for the Lord! ¹⁷ *They keep saying to those who despise My word, 'Don't worry! The Lord says you will have peace!' And to those who stubbornly follow their own desires, they say, 'No harm will come your way!'* ¹⁸ *"Have any of these prophets been in the Lord's presence to hear what he is really saying? Has even one of them cared enough to listen?* ¹⁹ *Look! The Lord's anger bursts out like a storm, a whirlwind that swirls down on the heads of the wicked.* ²⁰ *The anger of the Lord will not diminish until it has finished all he has planned. In the days to come you will understand all this very clearly.*

²¹ *"I have not sent these prophets, yet they run around claiming to speak for me. I have given them no message, yet they go on prophesying.* ²² *If they had stood before me and listened to me, they would have spoken My words, and they would have turned My people from their evil ways and deeds.* ²³ *Am I a God who is only close at hand?" says the Lord. "No, I am far away at the same time.* ²⁴ *Can anyone hide from me in a secret place? Am I not everywhere in all the heavens and earth?" says the Lord.* ²⁵ *"I have heard these prophets say, 'Listen to the dream I had from God last night.' And then they proceed to tell lies in My name.* ²⁶ *How long will this go on? If they are prophets, they are prophets of deceit, inventing everything they say.*

²⁷ *By telling these false dreams, they are trying to get My people to forget me, just as their ancestors did by worshiping the idols of Baal.* ²⁸ *"Let these false prophets tell their dreams, but let My true messengers faithfully proclaim My every word. There is a difference between straw and grain!* ²⁹ *Does not My word burn like fire?" says the Lord. "Is it not like a mighty hammer that smashes a rock to pieces?* ³⁰ *"Therefore," says the Lord, "I am against these prophets*

who steal messages from each other and claim they are from me. *31* I am against these smooth-tongued prophets who say, 'This prophecy is from the Lord!' *32* I am against these false prophets. Their imaginary dreams are flagrant lies that lead My people into sin. I did not send or appoint them, and they have no message at all for My people. I, the Lord have spoken!

False Prophecies and False Prophets

33 "Suppose one of the people or one of the prophets or priests asks you, 'What prophecy has the Lord burdened you with now?' You must reply, 'You are the burden! The Lord says he will abandon you! *'34* "If any prophet, priest, or anyone else says, 'I have a prophecy from the Lord,' I will punish that person along with his entire family. *35* You should keep asking each other, 'What is the Lord's answer?' or 'What is the Lord saying?' *36* But stop using this phrase, 'prophecy from the Lord.' For people are using it to give authority to their own ideas, turning upside down the words of our God, the living God, the Lord of Heaven's Armies. *37* "This is what you should say to the prophets: 'What is the Lord's answer?' or 'What is the Lord saying?' *38* But suppose they respond, 'This is a prophecy from the Lord!' Then you should say, 'This is what the Lord says: Because you have used this phrase, "prophecy from the Lord," even though I warned you not to use it, *39* I will forget you completely. I will expel you from My presence, along with this city that I gave to you and your ancestors. *40* And I will make you an object of ridicule, and your name will be infamous throughout the ages.'"

The Lord said;

You were correct when you said that everyone and their dog has risen and claimed a man given title, but I am the One who gave some to be prophets, some to be teachers, and some to be apostles. Man, in his arrogance, has given himself over to pride to promote himself. You are right not to call yourself a prophet;

it is not for you to call yourself that. It is a heavenly calling which others will recognize. They will recognize Me moving through you. You do not have to announce to the world, "I am a prophet," for how much more meaning and power does it contain when I reveal to the heart of man your calling?

Just as Jesus said to Peter, it is by the Spirit you know who I am.

When Jesus came to the region of Caesarea Philippi, He asked his disciples, "Who do people say that the Son of Man is?" "Well," they replied, "some say John the Baptist, some say Elijah, and others say Jeremiah or one of the other prophets." Then He asked them, "But who do you say I AM?" Simon Peter answered, "You are the Messiah, the Son of the living God." Jesus replied, "You are blessed, Simon son of John, because My Father in heaven has revealed this to you. You did not learn this from any human being. Now I say to you that you are Peter (which means 'rock'), and upon this rock I will build My church, and all the powers of hell will not conquer it. And I will give you the keys of the Kingdom of Heaven. Whatever you forbid on earth will be forbidden in heaven, and whatever you permit on earth will be permitted in heaven." **Matthew 13-19,**

I am the one who makes those revelations to the heart of those you come in contact with. You have made some mistakes as you have adjusted to the calling and learned to hear My voice, proclaiming My word as instructed. Each level will contain a learning curve, and you will learn to move in new levels of anointing, but have heart, I will never leave you or forsake you.

The words I have given you, I have spoken through Jeremiah for another generation. I now repeat them for this generation, who are out of line and out of order. Remove your titles, sons of man. Let *Me* bestow upon you the honor of your calling. Many will be angry and offended by this word, but offense is temporary, compared to an eternity spent paying for the mistakes of walking in error.

God have mercy, you cry. My church is out of line and out of touch; out of order, running this way and that, chasing the latest and greatest wisdom of man in pursuit of more of Me instead of investing time with Me, the very God from Whom they claim to want more. Distracted and in deception, they wander the highways and byways of the kingdom, never entering the court of the king, let alone the Holy of Holies to approach My throne.

There is a lot of talk. Talk is cheap. It is My presence that ushers in change; love, peace, and joy. The New Year will be a time of judgment and mercy, perfecting the saints to walk with Me and carry the anointing to greater levels. Your strength is needed, My light must shine out through darkness.

Repent now you "prophets" and titleholders. *I have not sent these prophets, yet they ran: I have not spoken to them, yet they prophesied. But if they had stood in My counsel, and had caused My people to hear My words, then they should have turned them from their evil way, and from the evil of their doings. AM I a God at hand, saith the LORD, and not a God afar off? Can any hide himself in secret places that I shall not see him? saith the LORD. Do not I fill heaven and earth? saith the LORD.*

I have heard what the prophets said, that prophesy lies in My name, saying, I have dreamed, I have dreamed. How long shall this be in the heart of the prophets that prophesy lies? Yea, they are prophets of the deceit of their own heart; Which thinks to cause My people to forget My name by their dreams, which they tell every man to his neighbor, as their fathers have forgotten My name for Baal. **Jeremiah 23:21-27.**

I have seen the folly of the prophets. They have caused My people to err. They have committed adultery in their hearts with titles and unclean things. They walk in lies, strengthening the hands of the evil ones, perverting the purity of My Holy Word. Do not listen, O' Israel. Do not listen, My children, for their words are in vain. Their words make you vain, lulling you into a false sense of security, tickling your ears with words of flattery and lies bent on your destruction. They speak words you want to hear, justifying your actions, your sins and your failure to seek My face.

They give a word from their own heart, not one from Mine. They cry peace but there shall be no peace; it is their desire for peace that prompts their words. No evil scheme shall befall you...carry on as you are...no one is judging you...but there *is* evil in this world, and their words lull you into a false sense of security.

Behold, a whirlwind of the Lord will go forth. A spiritual tornado, bringing winds of change to My house. The wicked will be caught up, and it will not cease until the desires of My heart have been satisfied. I am separating the wheat from the chaff, illuminating those who faithfully hear My Word. My Word is like fire; a hammer that cuts through the stony ground. Those who are stealing words, one from another are perpetuating lies and words of the heart of man; their tongue is saying, "Thus says the Lord," while they proclaim false words and false dreams, committing error by their lies and deception, trying to be "someone" in the kingdom ~ someone of importance, to have a self-imposed title. These are false dreams and visions. I did not send them. Their words of pachazuth, (frivolity, lightness), reckless and boasting joined with the words, "Thus saith the Lord," I did not send them.

People are asking, what saith the Lord? Has the Lord spoken? These people are not seeking to hear for themselves. I am against the prophets that steal words from their neighbor. I am against the false prophets that use their titles to claim I have spoken. I am against the prophets who prophesy false dreams to cause My people to err by pachazuth; substituting false words that rob My children of truth, as if they were from God, using their tongues, slander and false teachings, boasting of the divine calling, lightness, vanity, empty, and cheap talk. Just as some "prophets" proclaim lies as truth, others have proclaimed truth as lies. These false prophets turn God's solemn realities and words of judgment into mockery. Just as I address the ones who speak falsely, I will address those who claim the truth is false, for both are deadly to My body.

Your ears have been tickled to the point you cannot discern the truth from lies. My sheep hear My voice; so many voices are speaking. The only way to differentiate truth from the lies is by comparing it to the words I left you. Do not pick out one Scripture here and there to prove a point; allow Holy Spirit to lead and guide you in all truth, to differentiate what is truth from what is false. The false is everywhere, the counterfeit more real to some than truth. They defend it, perpetuate it, and never once consider they might be perpetuating lies of the evil one.

When confronted with truth, they cry loudly, "Do not judge." However, it is far better to be confronted with truth now while there is provision for forgiveness. One can sincerely be living and believing a lie. Come back to Me, My children, return to the basics of the faith.

Preach Christ. Christ born, Christ crucified, Christ resurrected. Preach baptism of the Holy Spirit, and watch things turn around. My hand of truth will prevail. Pride is rampant; no one is content to just serve Me, everyone wants to be somebody but the only "somebody" in the church should be the Father, Son, and Holy Spirit. Even My Son made Himself of no reputation. It is by Spirit that you are drawn to the Father, through the Son. Go in peace, My children. Walk circumspectly. Be as wise as serpents, and as innocent as doves.

December 18, 2011

LAND MINES

All eyes on Me. Do not deviate from what you hear the Spirit of the Lord saying. Follow His instructions to keep out of danger. Go right when He says go right, and left when He says go left, for this is crucial to your future. The road is tricky, paved with land mines to trip you up and blow up your way. Maneuvering around the land mines, which the enemy places before you, will take an acuteness of hearing. To maneuver through, keep your eyes on Me; tune your ears to hear what the Spirit of the Lord is saying.

Agility; The word for the New Year is agility. You must be willing to bend and change directions, swaying with fluidity, just as an ice skater moves along the ice.

Grace; This will be a year of strong shaking, but also a year of grace and favor on My chosen vessels. My chosen ones are a remnant of My people who remain, for such a time as this, to endure while proclaiming My name and My purposes. With unabashed abandon, you speak and seek My face, unafraid to proclaim My name and set the captives free.

Give Me praise. Praise your way through every situation, as praise opens doors you thought were closed, and closes doors you thought were open. I will guide you into your tomorrows. Speak, My children, speak. They will listen, not with their ears or their minds, but with their hearts. Their hearts hear what the Spirit of the Lord speaks through you. Their hearts respond because My name is written there. So speak in spite of the opposition and the persecution. Speak, for their hearts will hear and seeds will be planted, whether they realize it or not. There is power in the spoken word, especially when it lines up with My desires upon the earth and upon your lives. Speak children, speak. Change the circumstances around you as atmospheric changes ricochet off those things within earshot, changing destinies and penetrating hearts.

The Spirit of the Lord is moving. Do not hinder the work of the Spirit. Though land mines explode around you, and the noises are loud, with voices crying out, learn to hear Me through all the things that are vying for your attention. They are nothing but distractions. As significant as they feel, sound, and seem to be, they are nothing but distractions. See beyond the panic and fear. I will take your hand and maneuver you through the wreckage.

Hands; There will be hands, everywhere. Like a bad science fiction movie, they will be reaching out in every direction for help. Be My hands and feet. You have the answers to all predicaments. You have the answers to life itself. It can all be summed up in two words ~ Jesus Christ. I have spoken.

December 20, 2011

Vision:

MARTIAL LAW

The Lord gave Me a vision last night. I was in a sporting goods or military surplus type of store. I was looking for a certain item of clothing but could not find it as they were sold out.

Next I was in a two story house. I was standing on a balcony looking at a mountain in the distance. It looked like the big volcano in Japan.

I saw military in tanks with a man behind the machine gun. They used megaphones to announce that we had to remain inside, as they had declared Martial Law. There were troops walking the streets with automatic weapons. There were jeeps, tanks, Stryker vehicles, and helicopters all around.

I watched, fixated on the volcano despite the military presence everywhere. Suddenly, the top part of the volcano lifted up. I realized it was a huge "ship" or airplane (think the starship enterprise, only it was black with white "snow" on it and was disguised to look like the volcano/mountain). As it lifted up off the mountain, it left a huge crater. I realized that things we see are not what they seem. The aircraft began to fly. Shortly thereafter it was followed by hundreds of smaller ships.

Helicopters were flying by to help enforce martial law. There was a very *real* sense of danger. I went around talking, trying to comfort others in the house.

The Lord said the mountain was not what it seemed to be, neither are the things we are seeing and being told!! The mountain was massive, therefore significant things are not what they seem to be.

December 24, 2011

Vision:

THE WAVE

I woke at 2 a.m. At 2:13 a.m., the Lord showed me a vision.

I saw sky scrapers falling, then a huge wave of water carrying debris and people in its mix. I saw a man wearing a yarmulke and tallit, praying with his hands in the air. I watched this enormous wave hit him from behind, and he was swept away.

Pray. Pray for our Nation. Pray for our people. Pray for Israel.

I have had a similar wave vision before on the west coast, around Los Angeles. Based on what I saw in this vision the wave came from the east. I did not have a clear sense this day if it was meant to be literal, or spiritual.

I heard the Lord say, "When they cry peace and security, there will be instant destruction upon them."

Then He spoke the words, **Isaiah 42:6**; *I, the Lord, have called you in righteousness, and will hold your hand; I will give you as a covenant to the people, as a light to the Gentiles.*

December 28, 2011

Fresh Blessing

May the Lord bless you and keep you, may the Lord make His face to shine upon you, and may the Lord lift His countenance to you and give you peace (**Numbers 6:24-26**).

The above is greatest blessing ever recorded, yet I am about to bless My children in ways they never expected, ways they could never comprehend before this time in history. This will be necessary as My remnant, My called out ones, move and maneuver through this time in history. Ways you will not understand, ways that seem illogical, and almost detrimental at first blush, will usher in My plans and blessing that will allow you to fulfill your purpose in this next season.

There will be multiplication of resources; it will not look like enough, until you speak blessing over it. Raise your hands to heaven and receive the blessing of a fresh touch from the Holy One (author's note; when I did this as He was speaking, I felt warmth on My head and saw reddish smoke with glimpses of Lion of Judah, his eyes red with fire).

The warmth of My anointing is upon you, My child. I anoint your head with fresh oil and the warmth of My hand to bless nations. You will speak My Word, under My authority, to reach deaf ears and blind eyes with My good news, to see life transforming power unleashed in the lands. I speak Life. I speak blessing over you, for you are still a blessed and highly favored people. My remnant will survive the attacks, the many plots and the plans of our enemy (author's note; I am not sure this meant in the natural or just spiritual, based upon what He continued to speak). I will raise up My hand of protection and seal them with My name.

All of those who rise up against you, rise up against Me. My judgment will be swift in the land. It is the same as with Israel; those who rise up and bless will be blessed, and those who rise up and curse will be cursed, for My remnant children are the apple of My eye and My pride, and joy. Stand in My protection. Do not leave the hedge and wander off, for perilous times are here. Stay in the shadow of My wings, abiding in My presence where there is shelter from the storms protection from the rain, and the warmth of My presence in a cold world.

I seat you on high, a place of honor among nations. Along with honor comes jealousy and battles, for a servant is not greater than his master. As I sit in a place of honor in high places, I am hated, and the world will hate you for My namesake.

Blessings and favor do not always look like you think. Some of the most blessed were the most hated by the world for My sake. They were beaten and murdered for My name, as it will be with many of you. As the world changes and moves away from Me, know I am with you always, lo, to the end of the age. You are not alone, and when they lie to you, cheat you, hurt you, and slander your name, know they did it to Me, your Master, first. I will weep right along with you.

My Angels are alongside you for these things must come upon the Earth before My return. So know, My children, I will never leave you nor forsake you, even if it feels that way, or the enemy is speaking this to you. I will *not* leave My children. I will see you through the darkness to come, faithfully leading you home. I am waiting with open arms, for My kingdom belongs to all who overcome the world. Praise My Holy Name! Take an account, and count it ALL as your joy, for I have your hand secure.

December 30, 2011

BALANCE

I am the Lord your God, and I cast your cares as far as the east is from the west, for My burden is light. I have promised to never leave you or forsake you. I promised to provide for you, yet you doubt My word. Have I ever failed you in the past? You are still here, and your life is in the palm of My hand.

You may not always understand, but My grace is sufficient to carry you through the hard times and the trials of life. I will never leave you nor forsake you. I will never break covenant with you. My promises are yes and amen. My blessings are irrevocable, as you abide in Me.

My child, every good gift comes from My hand. I even give seed to the sower. I have built a kingdom around a covenant people, a promise. I have given My all. Everything you have comes from My hand. Every breath that you take and every beat of your heart is a connection to My Spirit. I teach you to give of yourselves the way I gave of Myself, to give of your heart, your hand, your life, by being that example to you. I am a giver; a God who gives, even though I also take away to make room for more of Me. I am a God who removes distractions and other things which hamper your relationship with Me.

I am shaking. This is a time of shaking, allowed to bring things back into balance in your life. You need balance of My word, balance in the Spirit, balance in the natural, and balance in the gifts. Balance allows rekindling of the flame within you.; it is a flame of fire and passion, restoring you to your first love, igniting a blaze that spreads zeal to those around you. These flames will fuel the passion of My presence, My word, and My Spirit, reviving the dead places, dead people, dead cities and land; even the parched and dry places in your own heart.

Receive the fire. Raise your hands to receive the fire. Raise your hands to Heaven and receive turnarounds and restoration as you move back into balance. Extremes in teachings have led many astray; countless are in danger, too far afield, jumping from one extreme to the next. I am not a God of extremes. I change not. Lift your hands to Heaven and ask for discernment; subtle deceptions are everywhere, and subtle deceptions are as dangerous, or more dangerous, than blatant extremes. Subtle deceptions sound right, almost comforting, but are destructive to your spirit and they lead to more and more corruption and compromise. A little leaven here, a little leaven there...a little leaven spoils the whole lump. Just as yeast causes the dough to rise, the distortions grow to larger and larger proportions. Guard your heart and your mind. Be stable and single minded.

Be as gentle as doves, but wise as serpents. The enemy is cunning and looking for whom he can destroy. Be careful, My children. Do not defend the indefensible. Do not compromise My values and My word. Do not make excuses for the sins of others. Do not make excuses or exceptions for falsehood, lies, and deceit.

My leaders must be beyond reproach. Test their words. Do not receive all that you hear. Do not bind yourself to the ministries of man, but to the ministry of Jesus Christ. Do not allow man to usurp your allegiance to Me. Remember Whom you serve. It is I, your God, not man. Stop making excuses for the wrong teachings of man. Do not perpetuate lies or skewed doctrine. Proclaim Jesus Christ in all things. Point to My glorious return when the earth, My footstool, and all things in it will be brought into submission under My ruling authority. Speak truth, walk in truth, do not lie.

Bear Witness Ministries

Contact Information:

www.bearwitnessministries.org

www.praisinginthepark.com

Book Store: www.bearwitnessbooks.com

youtube.com channel: bearwitnessmin or search Bear Witness Ministries

Facebook link for Kerrie/Bear Witness Ministries https://www.facebook.com/#!/bearwitnessministries

ABOUT THE AUTHOR

Kerrie Bradshaw is a bondservant of the Lord, Jesus Christ, and fellow laborer with the saints, who lives in Yucaipa, CA. Kerrie became a registered nurse in 1979, having completed her Bachelor of Science in Nursing (BSN) in 1981. In 1988, she launched *Medically Speaking*, a successful medical legal consulting business. Additionally, together with her husband, Bill, she Pastors Bear Witness Ministries and Praising in the Park. Praising in the Park is a weekly summer gathering that brings praise, worship and a Rhema/prophetic word to a public setting.

Born Jewish, and believing in God all her life, Kerrie received Jesus as Lord and Savior when she was 19 years old. The Lord moved in her life in a dramatic and powerful way in 2001, and has personally taught her the ins and outs of His Word, His Spirit, and His Truth through dreams, visions and prophetic gifts. He has endowed her with an amazing sensitivity to His voice. Many of the words contained in this book were dictated from Holy Spirit; He has given her a heart that parallels God's in its crying out for people to hear Him and know His truth, that they might be saved from eternal death.

In addition to her daily work, Kerrie has raised 14 children (four of her own, and 10 she and her husband took in). She has also led a community youth group, ministering to disadvantaged teens. It is one of her prayers that proceeds from the sale of her books will help her realize the dream of building a Teen Center/Youth Church in her hometown.

www.ingramcontent.com/pod-product-compliance
Lightning Source LLC
Chambersburg PA
CBHW051816090426
42736CB00011B/1510